GENERAL EDUCATION ASSESSMENT FOR IMPROVEMENT OF STUDENT ACADEMIC ACHIEVEMENT:

Guidance for Academic Departments and Committees

GENERAL EDUCATION ASSESSMENT FOR IMPROVEMENT OF STUDENT ACADEMIC ACHIEVEMENT:
Guidance for Academic Departments and Committees

by
James O. Nichols
Director Emeritus, University Planning and Institutional Research, University of Mississippi

and

Karen W. Nichols
Executive Director, Institutional Effectiveness Associates

AGATHON PRESS
New York

AGATHON PRESS
5648 Riverdale Avenue
Bronx, NY 10471

Library of Congress Cataloging-in-Publication Data:
Nichols, James 0. (James Oliver), 1941-
    General education assessment for improvement of student academic achievement: guidance for academic departments and committees / by James 0. Nichols and Karen W. Nichols.
    p. cm.
    ISBN 0-87586-133-4
    1. Universities and colleges--United States--Examinations--Handbooks, manuals, etc. 2. General education--United States--Evaluation--Handbooks, manuals, etc. 3. Academic achievement--United States--Handbooks, manuals, etc. I. Nichols, Karen W. II. Title

LB2366.2 .N53 2001
378.1'662--dc21

                        2001022152

CONTENTS

Figures

PREFACE

General education is the one common curricular component that all institutions of higher learning (except graduate and professional schools) share. This uniquely American curricular form is also known as the "core curriculum" and is among the common interests of regional accreditation associations throughout the United States. It is also the area that is most likely at public institutions to be the subject of "assessment for accountability" efforts on the part of the public or their representatives.

Assessment of general education normally takes place within the context of the overall institutional effectiveness/assessment activities described in *A Practitioners Handbook for Institutional Effectiveness and Student Outcomes Assessment Implementation,* third edition (1995). It is accomplished concurrently with assessment in the major or educational programs, as well as assessment in educational support and administrative units. These are described in *The Departmental Guide and Record Book for Student Outcomes Assessment and Institutional Effectiveness* published by Agathon Press in its third edition in 2000 as well as the new *Department Heads Guide for Assessment Implementation in Administrative and Educational Support Units,* also published by Agathon in 2000.

This monograph completes the series of program/unit level guides concerning specific types of assessment (majors, educational support and administrative units, and general education) likely within an institution of higher learning. It is very user-oriented; it is intended not as a scholarly work but rather as a practical guide for the individual or committee on a campus charged with assessing the institution's general education program. Institutions are encouraged to adjust and adapt the model described to best meet their institutional circumstances and culture.

The term "outcomes" utilized in this monograph, as well as in other publications, has a particular meaning. It refers to the *intended* or *expected* results of the instructional process as depicted in the column headed "Program Intended Educational Outcomes" in the two-, three-, four-, and five-column models illustrated in this publication. These intended or expected outcomes often stand in stark contrast to the *actual* or *realized* outcomes shown in the four- and five-column models depicted here.

Over the last dozen years, the authors have assisted almost two hundred institutions, from major research universities to two-year colleges, in the implementation of institutional effectiveness/assessment activities. During the course of that service, assessment in general education has repeatedly been addressed. This experience of working with faculty actually grappling with the challenge of assessment in general education formed the basis for this publication. Specific examples of models of general education assessment activities (through use of results to improve student learning) are provided for a comprehensive community college, a major state university, and a private college. Each of these models is designed to capture the culture of these institutions as they dealt with the issue of assessment in general education.

If comprehensive assessment of institutional effectiveness is to be successfully implemented on your campus, assessment of general education must be addressed. This monograph is designed to support that effort.

James 0. Nichols, Karen W Nichols
January 2001

CHAPTER I

DEFINING GENERAL EDUCATION AND THE ISSUES SURROUNDING ITS ASSESSMENT

General Education: A Definition

General education relates to the concept of communication of a common body of knowledge, skills and perspectives/values regarding civilization from one generation to another. Many describe general education as the "liberal arts" component of a curriculum containing what every graduate of the institution should be able to think, know, or do. Hence, in many ways, general education is the common denominator defining what students should accomplish while in attendance at an institution.

General education is also known on some campuses as the "core curriculum." It is frequently composed of between 24 and 56 semester credit hours in a baccalaureate program, or slightly less than one-half of a student's classes at a four-year institution. On most campuses, general education is composed of a series of classes which all students are required to take (English composition, math, etc.) and also a set of "distribution requirements" in other areas from which students choose electives to "round out" or individualize their general education experience. General education, or the core curriculum, does not include remedial or developmental programming or courses offered in direct support of a major (organic chemistry, anatomy and physiology, business math, etc.) offered by traditional liberal arts departments.

General education can be seen as the foundation upon which the rest of the baccalaureate level programming is based (see Figure 1). This foundation of liberal arts or general education courses for the four-year degree also provides the substance for two-year college "college parallel" programs. This programming at the two-year college is designed to provide the foundation upon which successful transfer to the four-year college is anticipated.

Another form of general education also is required of two-year occupational/technical students in community colleges. This form of general education is much briefer (normally six to twelve semester credit hours) and more focused upon support of the occupational/technical program (industrial math, business letter writing, etc.) than is the general education component of the college parallel program described in this publication.

Figure 1

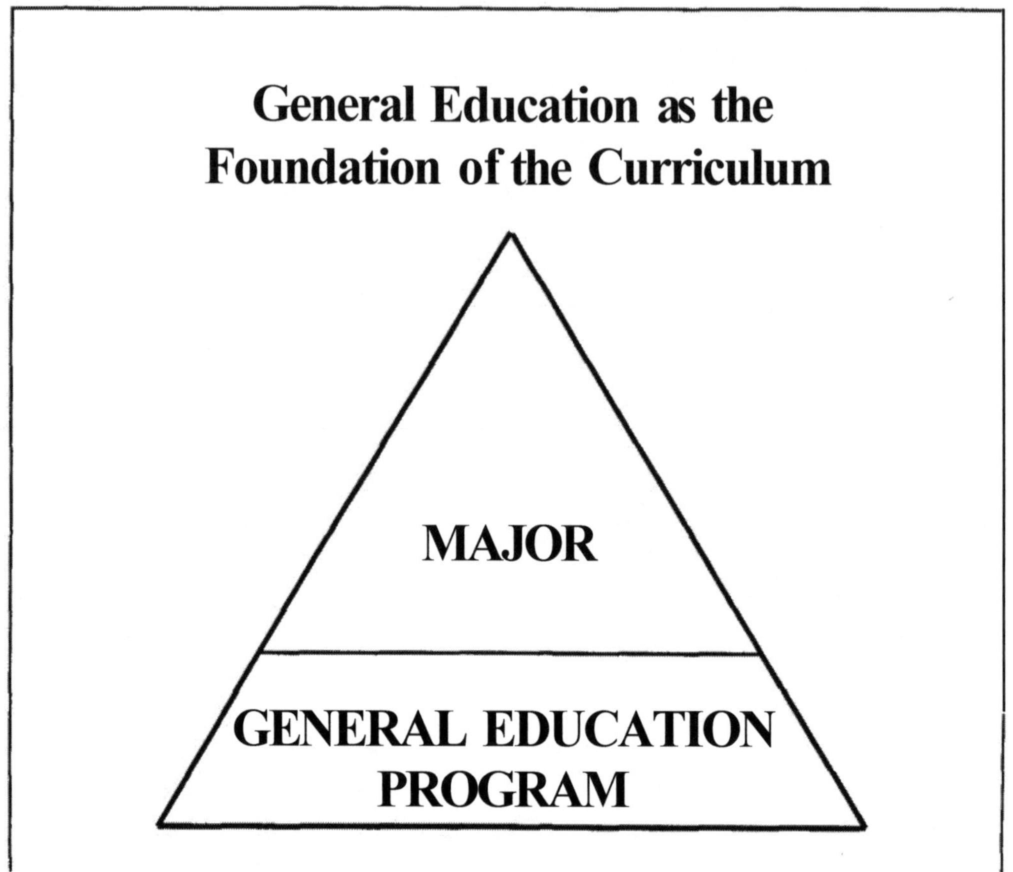

Issues in General Education and Its Assessment

Assessment in general education is, in the authors' opinion, the single most controversial assessment area on any campus. This is so for a number of reasons, among them the large size of the general education program as a proportion of the total curriculum, regional accrediting association attention, and state accountability requirements for general education found in many states.

There is no portion of the undergraduate curriculum that consumes as much time or resources as does the general education or core curriculum program on most campuses. Most undergraduate majors require 30-36 hours of course work, usually in a single department; however, the general education program on any campus exceeds that amount, though the impact of the general education program is dispersed across many departments offering "service courses." Many departments in liberal arts teach almost exclusively such "service courses" and in fact, owe their existence to the requirement for "service courses."

General education has always been a primary concern of regional accrediting associations and this interest has also been expressed in their assessment requirements. The publication provided to new visiting team members by the Commission on Colleges, Southern Association of Colleges and Schools, suggests questions to be raised regarding each portion of their *Criteria for Accreditation*. The first suggestion regarding Section III, Institutional Effectiveness, of the *Criteria for Accreditation* is "Ask them (the institution) about assessment in general education."

The Commission on Institutions of Higher Education, North Central Association of Colleges and Schools (NCA), demonstrated an abiding interest in general education long before assessment activities were ever considered. This interest was reflected in their requirement that assessment plans submitted by NCA institutions in 1995 include a component regarding assessment in general education. Further, activities regarding assessment in general education were described among those "Patterns of Evidence" which the Commission on Institutions of Higher Education, North Central Association of Colleges and Schools believes describe an institution in compliance with its requirements concerning assessment of student academic achievement.

One of the last regional accrediting associations on the "assessment band-wagon," is the New England Association of Colleges and Schools. The New England Association has made assessment of general education the centerpiece in its assessment implementation strategy and describes the composition of general education skills, knowledge, and perspectives/values in the most specific terms of any of the regional accrediting associations.

The number of state accountability requirements regarding assessment of general education seems to grow annually. This is a logical extension of the public's concern regarding whether their offspring (upon completion of K-12 and higher education) can read, write and do basic mathematical calculations. All too often, the public's impression is that the answer to these questions is not favorable. This has resulted in the requirement for state-mandated general education tests for all public higher education institutions in a number of states (Tennessee, Florida and Arkansas among others). In some cases, institutional input has been sought concerning identification of the particular instrument required; in others, external agencies such as governing boards and legislatures have mandated particular general education assessment instrumentation with little regard for institutional input or curriculum.

Accountability requirements have resulted in a mixed blessing for assessment at public institutions within their states. On the one hand, these institutions have seen that assessment actually took place to fulfill state requirements and in some states leverage to insure student motivation to take these general education instruments seriously has been created. On the other hand, the presence of state *accountability* focused assessment activities has often served as a substantial impediment to actual use of these assessment results by the faculty to *improve* general education activities on the campus and raised a number of **external issues**. This has been the case for several reasons. First, the identification of a single statewide general education standardized instrument removed from the faculty the authority to identify the means of assessment for general education and diminished their positive identification with the measure "forced" upon them. Thus, faculty's willingness to accept the results of such an instrument as a meaningful measure of their general education program has been undermined from the outset. Second, the existence of such a statewide standard means of general education assessment utilized to reward or punish institutions makes most faculty believe that assessment is indeed a "game" which the administration should play in order to acquire resources for the institution and is not of concern to them. Third, the existence of required general education activities serves as an excuse for not accomplishing genuine general educational assessment and absorbs most of the energy which might otherwise have been directed toward program improvement. The authors have first-hand experience with this situation on several campuses.

The **internal issues** in general education and assessment of student academic achievement in this field are legion. They include the variety of opinions concerning the subject, the subjective nature/value orientation of many of the concepts, the focus in liberal arts, relationship to professional school requirements, cross departmental linkages and turf protection (see Figure 2).

Figure 2

Internal or Campus Issues in General Education Assessment

- Variety of Opinions

- Subjective Nature/Value Orientation

- Focus in Liberal Arts Disciplines without Assessment Experience

- Relationship to Professional School Requirements

- Cross Departmental Linkages

- Prominence of "Turf Protection"

Unlike assessment in the major, there is little beyond the basic skills of "reading, writing and arithmetic" that constitute the common wisdom regarding general education on any campus. There are probably as many opinions regarding what constitutes general education as there are faculty, staff and students at any campus. This is very unlike the circumstance in most majors in which a common or accepted body of knowledge regarding the subject (with minor variance from institution to institution and between faculty members) exists. In general education, there is relatively little agreement regarding what constitutes general education and great variance of opinion from institution to institution and individual to individual.

A great deal of this difference of opinion relates to the subjective/value orientation of many of the intended outcomes associated with general education. Critical thinking, altruism, belief in the democratic ideal, diversity, social consciousness, are all subjects of importance on one campus or another and yet are often at best ill-defined even on those campuses where they are identified as an intended outcome. Particularly on campuses with a religious affiliation and intent to pass on this heritage and system of beliefs to future generations, these subjective or value-oriented outcomes are important and yet are often not consistently understood. The assessment or measurement of the extent of the accomplishment of these subjective and frequently ill-defined outcomes further complicates the issue. In most cases, asking clients or graduates whether they have acquired the value identified (ethics) results in the only socially acceptable response. This challenges campuses to identify other means for assessment of these outcomes and in the process to create an operational or working definition of what had been previously considered the ineffable.

The focus of most general education outcomes and their assessment in the liberal arts create further campus obstacles to implementation. Many of the faculty in the liberal arts are, by the nature of their discipline, philosophically opposed to the concept of stating outcomes, conducting assessment, and using the results for program improvement. Hence, there is often not a willing audience in some aspects of the liberal arts (humanities, fine arts, etc.). Also, liberal arts departments rarely have experience in professional accreditation requiring assessment for their majors which professional schools have undergone.

Further complicating general education within the university environment in which professional schools exist is the relationship between the requirements of the professional schools (expressed in numbers of credit hours in the field and now in terms of outcomes in some professional accreditation requirements) and the general education curriculum. Dynamic tension between these two competing forces (the focus on general education vs. the focus on the major in the professional schools) is of long standing. It has ebbed and flowed during the past fifty years. What is new in this regard is the expectation on the part of many professional accrediting associations that students in the professional schools will be able to demonstrate the skills such as verbal and written communications that should have been developed during their general education program in courses taught primarily by the liberal arts faculty. This contributes directly to the fifth campus assessment issue described below.

The fifth internal campus issue in assessment of general education is the need to work across departmental, college, or school boundaries in many assessment activities. Within higher education, we (faculty) work fairly well within our own academic departments, but it is somewhat unusual to find faculty working well with faculty in other departments who often use different terminology and approaches in problem solving. In many cases, institutions have overcome this reluctance through the extensive use of cross-departmental task forces or committees on a variety of topics.

One of the principal campus issues in general education assessment is "turf protection." Unlike assessment in the major, where the impact of changes in the curriculum remain relatively isolated within the department housing the major, changes or adjustments in the general education curriculum echo across departmental lines and because of the volume of students taking general education courses can bring about a substantial impact upon faculty staffing across departments. As an example, should the institution's assessment activities indicate the need for an additional quarter or semester of mathematics instruction in order to bring students' performance in mathematics to the level that the faculty in the math department and the general education committee believe that it ought to attain, it may be necessary to employ a number of additional math faculty. Assuming the institution is at a steady state in funding, these additional faculty positions that are going to the mathematics department will come from vacant positions in other departments. Faculty are not slow to identify this relationship and often reflect this in strong opposition to the need for curricular change. While this certainly is not the high road toward curricular reform or refinement, it is one often encountered on campuses.

Transfer v.s. General Education at the Two-Year College

On two-year college campuses, the relationship between the "transfer program" and the "general education program" also constitutes an issue to be resolved. While the bulk of students preparing to transfer to a four-year institution take the general education or college parallel curriculum, the merger of transfer and general education into a single entity for assessment purposes has proven confusing on many two-year college campuses. It is recommended that separate assessment plans and documentation be prepared for *that which students enrolled in the college parallel curriculum learn or the skills which they acquire while in attendance at the two-year college—the general education program,* and, separately, *the experience of two-year college transfer students at the four-year institutions to which they transfer—the transfer program.* Hence, general education assessment focuses internally within the institution on the learning and skills acquired while in attendance at the two-year college while the transfer program assessment structure focuses upon students' success once enrolled in the four-year institution.

Having briefly defined general education and identified its myriad of issues, nonetheless assessment of student academic achievement in this area is a reality which every institution must face. In the following chapter this reality is addressed by discussion of the approaches to assessment of general education and structure through which this activity should take place.

CHAPTER II

APPROACHES TO THE ORGANIZATION AND ASSESSMENT OF GENERAL EDUCATION

Structure of Assessment Activities

Unlike assessment in the major, where there is a specific body of knowledge or skills and faculty committed to the discipline, general education is a difficult subject to approach because of its varied composition and the general lack of faculty identification with the field. On many campuses, if you send out a notice asking to meet with the "general education faculty" you will find no one attends. However, if you call a meeting with the Department of English or the Department of Math, etc., faculty will attend because of their identification with the subject matter. The point, simply, is that it is difficult to approach assessment of general education because on most campuses there is no group of faculty that identifies first with general education and second with their discipline. The order of allegiance is first with their department and then (perhaps) with general education.

From the authors' experiences, there appear to be two basic approaches to the organization and assessment of general education. These are the *programmatic* approach and the *departmental/course* approach. The programmatic approach conceptualizes general education as a coordinated whole leading to the development of the *overall* student as a member of society. The departmental/course approach sees general education as a loose collection of courses from each discipline with a wide selection of distribution requirements. The programmatic approach leads to program level outcomes and assessment while the departmental/course approach may flow from some overreaching programmatic outcomes, but focus on course level objectives and assessment thereof. The departmental/course approach to general education organization and assessment is, in the experience of the authors, the more commonly chosen approach. It offers a familiar structure for faculty members, (their own department) and course level assessment is apparently easier to accomplish "one course at a time."

The disadvantages which lead to the failure (in most cases) of the departmental or course level approach to assessment are numerous. First, this approach fails to consider the development of the individual "as a whole" (often after describing a general education program focused upon development of the "well rounded" or

Figure 3

The Course Level Approach
to Assessment of General Education
GENERAL EDUCATION OUTCOMES:
Writing Skills
Oral Communications
Analytical Skills
Course:
Objectives:
Assessment:
THROUGH
THROUGH
THROUGH
English 141
Political Science 111
Math 121
Research Paper
Historical Perspective Project
Common Course Exam

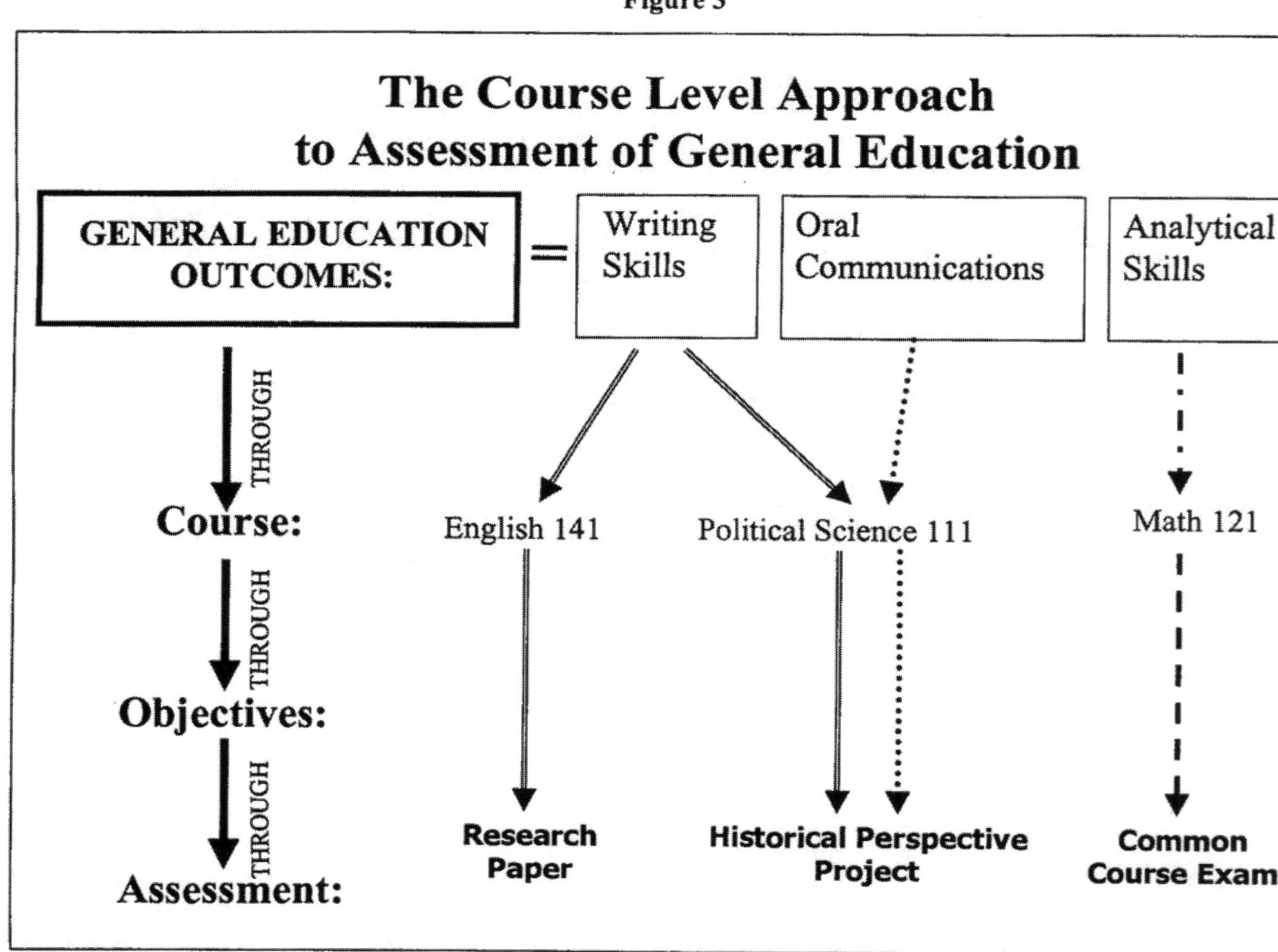

"whole" student in its mission statement, catalog, and/or recruiting material). Second, this approach leads to the need to establish a relationship between course objectives and program outcomes and requires assessment of the achievement of course objectives by more than the individual faculty member teaching the course (see Figure 3). Third, this approach generally does not fit well with regional accreditation requirements which speak to the overall general education program. Finally, and most emphatically, *the departmental or course level approach to general education assessment generates a level of assessment work at the course level which is so resource and labor intensive that it can not be sustained for any meaningful period of time*. The result of institutions choosing this course of action is most often exhaustion and disappointment on the part of the faculty involved with little meaningful change or improvement in learning.

Frequently, the authors have visited campuses where it has been possible to conduct assessment of writing and mathematical skills at the close of courses in these subjects. That ability, combined with indifference toward and lack of identification with the discipline of "general education," has led faculty to limit assessment in general education to the department/course level approach in only math and writing. This decision results in failure to ever consider assessment beyond the most basic skills and thereby trivializes this important subject.

The programmatic approach considers general education as a whole with identifiable outcomes and different disciplines contributing to each of those outcomes (see Figure 4). The principal advantages of this approach are: (a) its comprehensive treatment of the subject, (b) its facilitation of assessment "beyond the individual section and instructor level," (c) its feasibility for implementation within an achievable and sustainable level of effort, and (d) the extent to which this approach fits most regional accrediting association expectations.

The primary disadvantage of the program level approach to general education assessment is the need to work across departmental (and college/school) lines which many campuses lack experience in doing. Without the existence of a previous track record or history of working cooperatively on general education, the likelihood of choosing this programmatic approach to assessment of general education is substantially reduced. The programmatic approach to assessment of general education is, regretfully, "the road less taken."

The discussion above concerning approaches to assessment of general education addresses the issue of these activities at either the *program* or *course* level. There are few things which can be promised in assessment activities of any type. However, one is that faculty at most institutions will not implement comprehensive course level assessment activities over a sustained period of time. While, theoretically attractive, this route leads institutions to "choke and die" on the assessment effort which they have created for themselves. On the other hand, program level or programmatic assessment of general education is distinctly accomplishable and sustainable year in and year out.

It is our recommendation (based upon twelve years of experience working with

approximately 200 institutions) that your campus accept the programmatic approach to assessment of general education and its challenge to work together toward a unified and improved curriculum in this important area. The balance of this monograph is based upon the assumption of a programmatic approach to general education and its assessment.

Figure 4

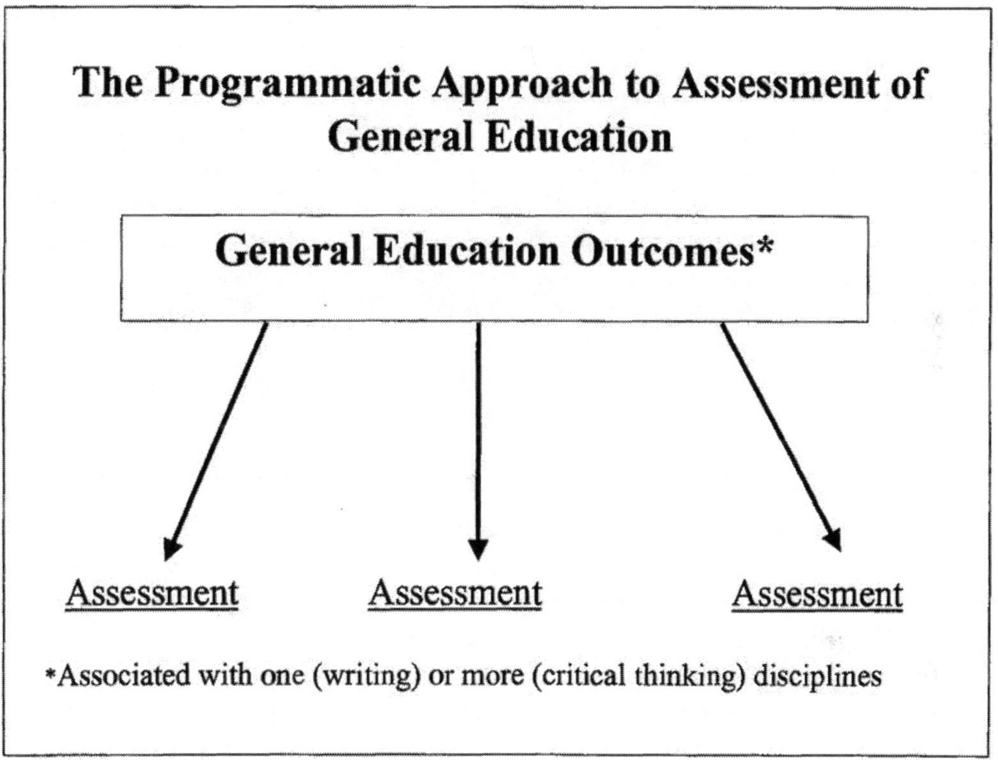

Coordination of General Education Assessment

Coordination, administration, direction, or responsibility for general education on most campuses is an orphan. Though this component of undergraduate education constitutes in most cases, nearly half of a student's undergraduate curriculum, institutions seldom effectively oversee their general education or core curriculum program.

At one time in the mid-twentieth century, the notion of a "general college" responsible for offering the courses taken in general education or the core curriculum became somewhat popular. The most noted example of this was the General College at the University of Minnesota. Under this structure, the dean of the general college had the overall responsibility for coordination or administration of the program. However, due to a number of factors, including difficulty in recruiting and retaining faculty (who are primarily related to their discipline), brought about a decline of this organizational structure throughout the balance of the century.

On some campuses, there exists a general education curriculum committee responsible for the coordination of these offerings. However, more frequently general education is assigned to the institutional "curriculum committee" as its responsibility. In either case, general education or core curriculum responsibility is exercised primarily through the individual academic departments responsible for providing the service courses. Under this scenario, frequently weak general education or curriculum committees are left to the tender mercies of more organized and committed faculties in the individual academic departments. Most of these departments are intent upon seeing that the maximum amount of their discipline is required in the general education program.

In many cases, the individual responsible for coordination, administration, etc., of the general education program is equally difficult to identify. While ultimate responsibility must lie with the institution's chief academic officer, that individual frequently passes authority (though not responsibility) for general education administration to an associate or assistant chief academic officer or to one of the committees referenced above. The most common answer the authors receive when asking the question on campuses, "Who is responsible for general education?" is (after a pause and some thought on the part of the respondent), "Well, I guess no one."

Given the fact that the party or group responsible for general education is difficult to identify, what group then should be responsible for *assessment* of general education? The answer lies in those identified as being responsible for coordination of general education, the institutional assessment committee, or a separate committee established for this purpose. The advantages of utilizing the *same group identified as responsible for general education* for its assessment include their familiarity with the subject, probable representativeness of the stakeholders involved, and their responsibility for identification of intended outcomes for the general education program.

The main disadvantage of having this original committee serve the purpose of coordinating general education assessment lies in the existing level of commitment or work on the part of the committee and their lack of knowledge of assessment procedures. In most instances, groups or individuals who have borne the responsibility for the general education committee and outcomes consider themselves already overcommitted by that act and have little interest in also dealing with assessment. In addition, many of these committee members will have little interest or expertise in assessment procedures.

Utilization of the *institutional assessment committee* also exhibits a number of advantages and disadvantages. The chief advantages of this approach lie in the current existence of the committee (thereby avoiding the appointment of another committee) and the relative expertise in assessment procedures being developed by its members. However, these advantages are more than offset by the disadvantages of this approach which include lack of representativeness of the primary stakeholders in general education, as well as the fact that the institutional assessment committee is already heavily committed to other actions. "Assessment" of general education is in most cases a "task unto itself."

The establishment of a *separate general education assessment committee* is probably the best approach to coordination of this important activity. One or more members of the institutional assessment committee can become the core of this committee and be augmented by the stakeholders from the primary service departments as well as campus "experts" in such fields as reading, mathematics, and writing. While this approach requires appointment of another committee, the committee's work can be linked through joint memberships to that of the institutional assessment committee. Its establishment allows the general education assessment committee to focus its attention solely on this important subject.

The identification of the general education outcomes often becomes a stumbling block for general education assessment. Sometimes this is because the curriculum for general education has been designed more by political gerrymandering of the departments and courses than by reason. Under these circumstances, the first issue, which an institution will need to accomplish, is identifying the outcomes served by the existing curriculum.

CHAPTER III

THE SUBSTANCE AND OUTCOMES OF GENERAL EDUCATION

General Education Description

The substance of general education (see page 11 for earlier definition) varies tremendously across and within institutions of higher learning. When viewed as a series of curriculum patterns, general education often includes communications, mathematics, humanities, behavioral and social sciences, and natural sciences (see Figure 5).

Figure 5

Curricular Patterns in General Education

- Communications

- Mathematics

- Humanities

- Behavioral and Social Science

- Natural Science

Curriculum patterns within "communications" most often relate to written and verbal communications. However, on some campuses, this field extends to communications through symbols and other means of non-verbal communication, as well as listening skills.

Within the field of mathematics, there is great variance from campus to campus concerning the level and type of mathematics curriculum through which students are asked to progress. On many campuses, these requirements include one or more levels of remedial or developmental mathematics prior to actually beginning the general education curriculum. Within mathematics, choices range from finite math to college algebra to calculus.

Within the humanities, students are often asked to navigate curricular patterns designed to communicate both a sense of historical or cultural perspective as well as the values of the culture. Other campuses blend humanities requirements with those of the social sciences.

Curricular patterns related to the behavioral and social sciences are indeed varied. Part of the curriculum in this area relates to the acquisition of a certain set of knowledge concerning the way in which individuals in society function while the single thread that seems to be consistently woven throughout these curricular patterns is the ability of the student to discern between alternative interpretations and values. This is, upon occasion, described as critical thinking.

There are no more diverse curricular patterns than those demonstrated by the natural sciences. However, the common concept among these sciences is their inclusion of the scientific method as a basis for their fields.

Regardless of the particular set of general education curricular patterns or requirements evidenced on a campus, there exists a number of externally imposed limitations and constraints on an institution's latitude in selection or design of its curriculum. The impact of the general education requirements of the four-year institutions to whom two-year college graduates transfer is of great influence on two-year college general education curricula. In many cases, students choose their curricular content based upon, not the two-year college's general education curriculum, but the requirements of the institution to which they intend to transfer. Two other external forces have substantial impact on the curricular patterns in general education on a campus. One of these forces acts to restrict the amount of general education required, and the other to expand it.

Professional school (and accrediting association) requirements concerning the number of hours required in the major directly impact the number of hours which may be dedicated to general education. This is a reflection of the conflicting philosophy of "specialization" versus "generalization" in curriculum design. If there are to be more hours focused in the specialization or in the major in response to the requirements of professional accreditation associations, there must necessarily be fewer hours devoted to general education unless the total number of hours for the baccalaureate degree is expanded beyond 128. Such an expansion would be opposed by most student groups and governing boards.

Partly in response to the above cited encroachment on curricular patterns in general education by professional accrediting associations, regional accrediting associations often dictate general education curricular patterns (see previous discussion on page 13). As an example, the Commission on Colleges, Southern Association of Colleges and Schools (SACS) requires 30 semester hours of general education for the baccalaureate degree and 15 semester hours for the associate degree. Additionally, SACS stipulates that these hours should be in the following fields, "humanities/fine arts, social behavioral/sciences, and natural sciences/ mathematics." The nature of the courses taken in the fulfillment of this requirement must not be specialized in nature such as mathematics for nurses, poetry for plumbers, psychology for social workers, public speaking for accountants, or the history of mathematics.

Typical General Education Outcomes

When viewed as the outcomes or results of general education, a taxonomy of general education **expected** outcomes might include basic skills, knowledge/understanding, higher order thinking, and values development (see Figure 6).

Figure 6

A Taxonomy of General Education Outcomes

- Basic Skills

- Knowledge/Understanding

- Higher Order Thinking Skills

- Values Development

The "basic skills" cited in most general education programs include: Reading, Writing, Speaking, Listening, Performing mathematical calculations, and Demonstrating basic computer skills (see Figure 7)

There is general agreement on most campuses concerning the need for graduates to have the ability to read, write and take part in oral communication. However, even in these most basic areas, the specific operational definition of these terms and the answer to the question: "How well should our graduates be expected to read, write, or speak?" is often not addressed.

The ability to perform basic mathematical calculations also is commonly accepted as a basic **intended outcome of general education**. The emphasis here is not on knowledge concerning the meaning of the mathematical calculations or their appropriateness for a particular end, but on the ability to conduct the calculations themselves.

Computer literacy is clearly emerging as a commonly accepted skill on campuses and in society. As in the cases above, it is in the definition of the term that most work remains to be accomplished. Computer literacy at a highly technical institution emphasizing engineering is quite a different concept than at a liberal arts college.

Figure 7

Typical Areas in Which <u>Basic Skills</u> Outcomes are Formulated

- Reading
- Writing
- Performing Mathematical Calculations
- Demonstrating Basic Computer Skills
- Speaking
- Listening

Less likely, but occasionally encountered, as **intended outcomes of general education** are the "life skills" espoused in the writings of John Dewey. These skills include interpersonal relations, self-knowledge, etc. The inclusion of these skills in general education was a more common phenomena in the past than in the present; however, their existence is certainly worthy of note.

In addition to the basic skills, it is anticipated that degree recipients will have a "knowledge/understanding" of common themes in the culture in which they will function (see Figure 8). Often the outcomes in this arena relate to students' knowledge of the past, which enables them to view events in historical perspective. This historical perspective may be amplified by students' familiarity with the literature and understanding of the literary styles encountered in each historical period. The joint impact of the students' historical perspective and knowledge of literary styles and the culture therein often are reflected in outcomes which seek to identify different philosophical approaches to life within the current society.

Among the more recent emphases in general education outcomes noted by the authors in their visits to campuses have been the increase in understanding of the meaning of numerical data and the existence of a global perspective on the part of students. As quantitative reasoning has increased as a basis for decision making, colleges are tending to place more emphasis upon the ability not only to conduct calculations, but also to understand the meaning of the resulting data or statistics. Also, an increasing number of institutions include in their general education outcomes the students' knowledge of their culture's place within the global village. The impact of technology and communications are often also emphasized in these types of outcomes.

Figure 8

Typical Areas in Which <u>Knowledge/ Understanding</u> Outcomes are Formulated

- Historical Perspective

- Literary Styles

- Culture

- Meaning of Numerical Data

- Global Perspective

- Impact of Technology

In addition to the "basic skills" and "knowledge or understanding" of the culture, many institutions include "higher order thinking skills" in their general education outcomes. Descriptions of these skills commonly include terms such as critical thinking, logical reasoning, scientific/abstract inquiry, and concept integration (see Figure 9). Each of these terms, while having specific and often different meanings in

Figure 9

Typical Areas in Which <u>Higher Order Thinking Skills</u> Outcomes are Formulated

- Critical Thinking

- Logical Reasoning

- Scientific/Abstract Inquiry

- Concept Integration

the jargon of various fields, share a great deal in common. They relate to an individual's ability to use scientific or other methodology to discern among alternatives through the use of either inductive or deductive reasoning. They are characterized as "skills of the mind" and cut across the curricular patterns described earlier. The skills can be utilized to integrate what otherwise appear to be disparate approaches to general education in the various disciplines.

"Values" related outcomes are unquestionably the most controversial and difficult outcomes to measure (see Figure 10). In public institutions, these outcomes frequently relate to students' development of a commitment to the democratic ideal or citizenship. Acceptance on the part of students of the desirability of cultural diversity or a pluralistic society is also common among such outcomes at public institutions.

Figure 10

Typical Areas in Which <u>Values Development</u> Outcomes are Formulated

- Commitment to Democratic Ideal

- Cultural Diversity

- Aesthetic Appreciation

- Ethical Perspective

- Religious Orientation

Both public and private institutions share some value-related educational outcomes. There are very few institutions that do not espouse the development of "aesthetic appreciation" by their graduates. However, the meaning of that term remains elusive on most campuses. Likewise, the development of an ethical perspective leading to the graduation of students with high moral or ethical standards is a commonly desired outcome at both public and private institutions. It is often in the specification of what "ethics" or moral standards are expected of students that public and private institutions are different.

The singular value whose development is restricted to denominationally related institutions is that of religious orientation. While some institutions with denominational relations seek merely to encourage their students toward belief in a "supreme being," others are unashamedly committed to their students' adoption of a particular religious doctrine. Either approach is entirely appropriate in a free society where students are able to choose the nature of their higher education.

Formulation of Intended Educational Outcomes Concerning General Education

Intended educational (student) outcomes concerning general education serve a number of purposes. The most important of these purposes is the articulation of the educational characteristics that we seek in generally or liberally educated students at the time of their completion of the general education curriculum. In addition, these outcomes serve important roles regarding validation of the institution's statement of purpose, engagement of the faculty, and the assessment process itself.

Statements of general education intended educational (student) outcomes should link to and support the institution's statement of purpose. On some occasions (see Figures 14 and 16 on pages 34 and 35, respectively) this linkage is most direct, as the institution will have included in its statement of purpose the educational characteristics it seeks in its graduates. This is not an uncommon event and under such circumstances institutions need to insure that the obligation created in their statement of purpose is followed through in the general education outcomes identified. In other cases (see Figure 15, page 34), linkage to the statement of purpose will be through a much more general reference to the undergraduate educational experience.

The formulation of educational outcomes is the first place that most faculty become involved in the institutional effectiveness or assessment endeavor. In the case of general education, outcomes formulation should result from consultation not only with those units traditionally providing service courses, but also with the faculty in the professional schools whose programs are built upon the general education curriculum.

The general education outcomes identified by the faculty are an important part of the assessment plan developed for the general education program. They focus assessment activities in general education on only those outcomes identified at any specific time as subject to evaluation or assessment. In addition, they create a strong market for the results of assessment activities which leads to program improvement.

It is important for faculty to understand that they are being asked to formulate statements of what students or graduates upon completion of general education will be able to think, know, or do, which are the "outcomes" of student learning, rather than statements concerning what the faculty intends to do as a part of the general education process (see Figure 11). This distinction between "process" and "outcomes" is often muddled in states having accountability related assessment initiatives. Often, from the state level, purely process oriented performance indicators such as number of graduates, number of enrollees or degrees awarded, etc., are utilized in conjunction with the term institutional effectiveness. These statements do not measure what students think, know or do and their substitution for measures of student learning or "outcomes" often leads to the establishment of assessment plans and procedures measuring the educational "process" rather than the result of that process, educated graduates. This is the first opportunity for general education faculty to "take the wrong fork in the road" resulting in an extremely disappointing journey to frustration.

Figure 11

Statements of General Education Outcomes

- **Should** reflect what *groups of students* can do upon completion of the general education curriculum

- **Should <u>not</u>** describe the activities of *faculty or academic departments* taking part in the general education process

Characteristics of Statements of Intended General Education Outcomes
Intended educational (student) outcomes concerning general education should be linked to the institutional statement of purpose, reasonable given the ability of students attending the institution, specific in nature, and limited in number to three to five intended outcomes upon which assessment is being conducted at any one time (see Figure 12). As mentioned earlier, it is important that the linkage of each general education outcome to the institution's expanded statement of institu-

Figure 12

Characteristics of Statements of Intended General Education Outcomes

- Linked to the Expanded Statement of Institutional Purpose

- Reasonable Given the Ability of the Students Admitted

- Specific in Nature

- For the Most Part, Quantifiable

- Limited in Number to 3-5 Being Assessed at Any One Time

tional purpose be established. This linkage will either be direct or indirect; however, it is this linkage process that turns what would otherwise be exclusively program evaluation into a measure of institutional effectiveness.

The statements of educational outcomes concerning general education should definitely take into account the nature of the incoming student body. It is unreasonable to expect that disadvantaged students from who enroll at a comprehensive community college or baccalaureate institution with open admissions will be able to overcome in two to four years the handicap of having spent twelve years in school systems that were unable to prepare them fully for postsecondary work. The faculty supporting the general education program need to establish a reasonable relationship between the nature of the student body admitted and the general education curriculum as well as the outcomes for that program.

General education intended educational outcomes need to be specific enough for subsequent assessment or evaluation. In so very many cases, general education intended outcomes are initially formulated in terms of what can only be described as "truth and beauty." The use of such terms as critical thinking, ethics, social consciousness, global perspective, commitment to diversity and cultural pluralism while certainly pleasing to the ear and the senses do not lend themselves well to measurement or evaluation. These terms, and others of a similar nature, carry substantially different meanings on any campus. This often intentional ambiguity is one of the reasons that such statements are established and find wide support among the faculty.

From an assessment standpoint, terms such as those referenced above must be refined to a more operational or measurable level in the means of assessment identified. What does the institution mean by "ethics?" Whose ethics? Based upon what value system? What do we mean by "critical thinking?" Do we mean inductive reasoning or deductive reasoning? Is critical thinking the ability to draw inference from a set of data? These types of discussions and questions characterize the need as one client remarked to "operationalize the ineffable."

Fortunately, it is not necessary to "operationalize the ineffable" to three decimal places. Usually, even difficult to measure outcomes such as those listed above can be brought to a point of general agreement regarding the success of the program in achieving its intentions. This is often accomplished through extended discussions and/or descriptions of what a person exhibiting the desired characteristic would "be like" or "do" while in attendance or after graduation. However, there are a limited number of worthy intended educational outcomes (particularly those emanating from private denominational institutions) that the authors acknowledge are close to being unassessable. It is our joint recommendation that no more than one of these outcomes be identified on the initial short list upon which assessment is to take place, but that the bulk of such outcomes be approached one at a time as the short list is updated.

While it is not uncommon that the faculty in general education can identify an almost unlimited number of intended general education outcomes, assessment should take place concerning no more than three to five of these outcomes at any one time. None of the regional accrediting associations require that *everything be assessed all the time*. Their requirements state that an institution must have a systematic assessment procedure in place. For that reason, visiting teams from these associations readily accept the necessity of institutions dealing with assessment of only a portion of their general education outcomes at any given time. To attempt to assess more than three to five general education outcomes at any one time will lead to faculty overload and the tendency to "crash and burn."

In the assessment of general education, there are basically two approaches to the identification of the three to five outcomes to be assessed. The institution may take the approach of selecting one theme for assessment in a given year, thereby going into considerable depth regarding the outcomes associated with that theme or concept. As an example, an institution could pick a theme such as "communications" in a given year and identify a number of general education outcomes concerning topics such as writing, oral communications, and listening for assessment during that period of time. In such an instance, a portion of those faculty (such as those in the Departments of English and Speech) engaged in the general education process will be exceptionally busy with assessment activities during that period while those in mathematics and the natural sciences would not be taking part in general education assessment activities at that time.

The other (and more commonly taken) approach to selection of general education outcomes for assessment is characterized by the selection of one outcome each from a wide variety of areas. This approach would include an outcome concerning perhaps communications, one concerning mathematical abilities, another concerning scientific reasoning and others broadly representative of the educational outcomes identified regarding general education. This approach assures that most curricular areas would be doing some assessment in any given year, but precludes any area's examination in depth. If selecting this approach, it is particularly important to remember to limit the number of outcomes being assessed in any year to five as the tendency will be to involve *all* disciplines every year.

It is suggested that the faculty involved in the general education program identify the "long list" of intended general education outcomes depicted in Figure 13 and then through either approach described above select the three to five for assessment at any one time. The "long list" should be maintained so that intended outcomes not initially selected for the "short list" and assessment at this time are not disregarded but reconsidered each time outcomes are identified. As intended outcomes are assessed and evidence of the institution's success in this regard is provided, originally selected general education outcomes should be returned to the long list and others moved from the long list to the short list for assessment purposes. This procedure demonstrates the institution's systematic approach to assessment of the achievement of general education outcomes.

In arriving at the short list of three to five intended general education outcomes upon which assessment will be conducted at any one time, it is important to be precise. If the outcomes identified are characterized by commas, semicolons or conjunctions, there is a very good chance that in an effort to be politically correct and inclusive of all disciplines, numbers 1, 37, and 52 from the long list have been combined into one complex and in general "bundled" outcome. This results in more work than humanly possible to achieve at the time assessment activities actually take place. The notion here is to *select* from the long list three to five individual outcomes for assessment at any one time.

Figure13

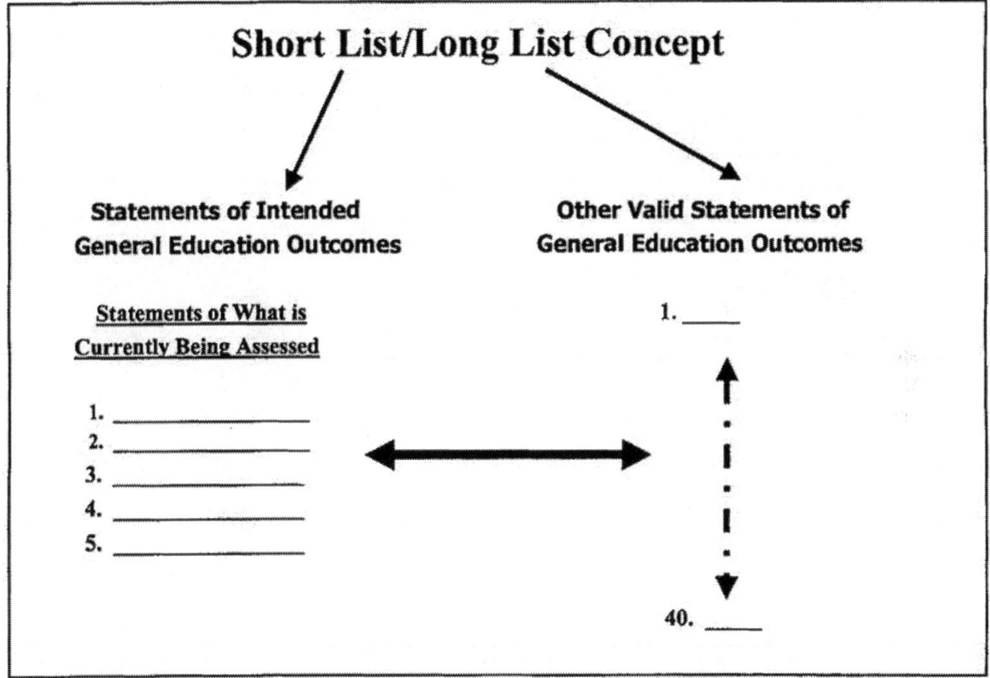

An institution can expect for its general education outcomes that are being assessed to shift back and forth between the long and short lists over a period of years. This demonstrates the dynamic nature of the process and illustrates to the visiting team members the institution's continuing commitment to improvement of student learning.

Concluding Comments and Examples of General Education Outcomes
The relationship between intended educational (student) outcomes for the general education program and the statement of purpose is depicted in the two-column models shown as Figures 14, 15, and 16 on the succeeding pages. These figures provide examples of the intended educational (student) outcomes for the college parallel, general education program at a comprehensive community college, as well as the general education program at a private institution, and a major public research university. These models will be developed throughout the rest of this publication to include not only the means of assessment identified for each of the educational outcomes formulated, but assessment data resulting from the implementation of these means of assessment, and, where appropriate, the use of results to improve general education programming.

Figure 14

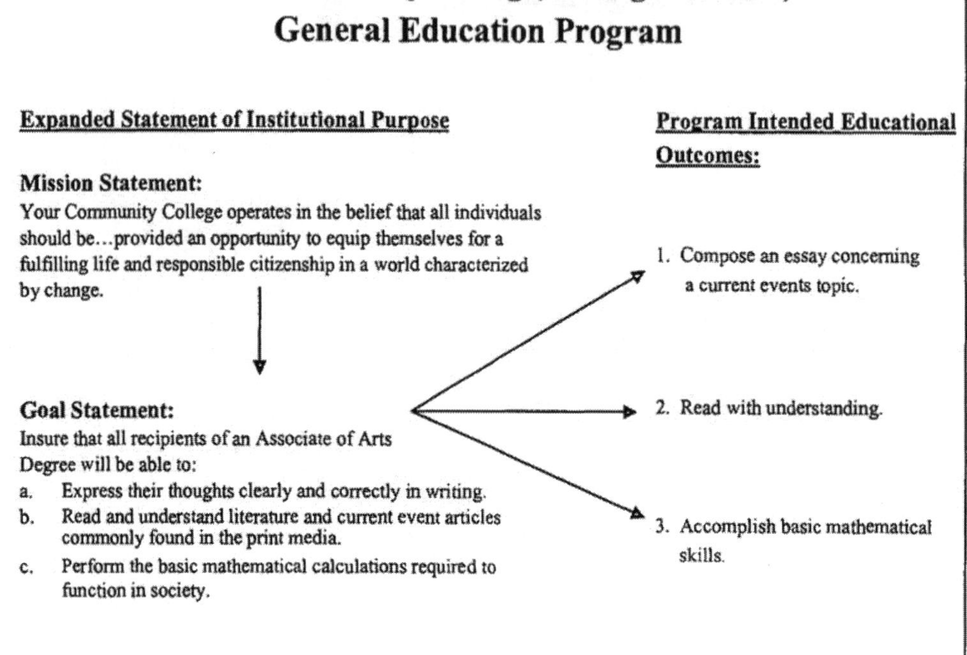

Figure 15

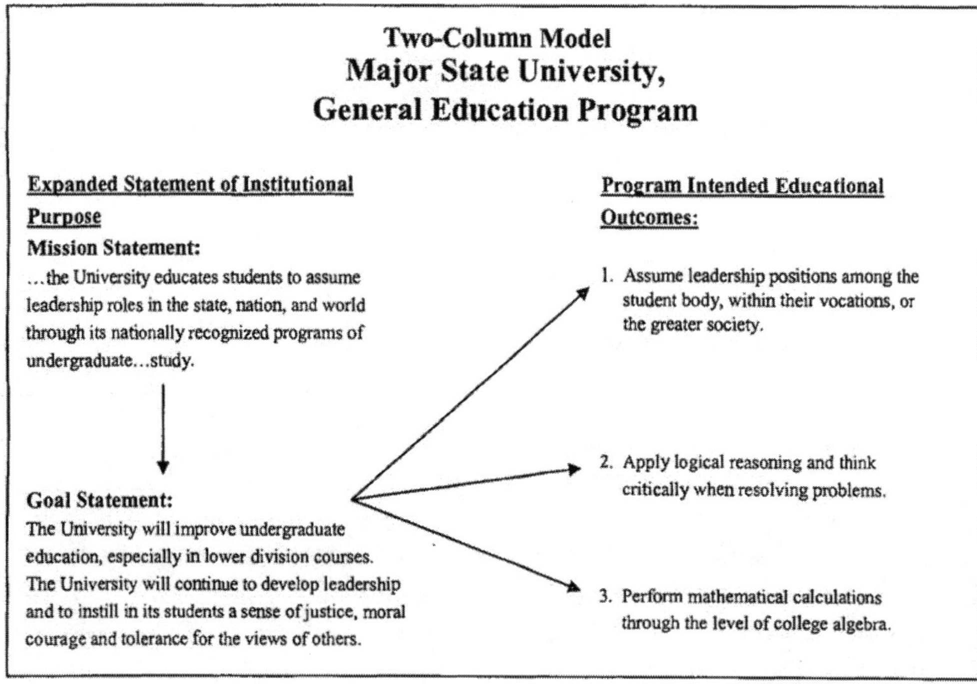

Figure 16

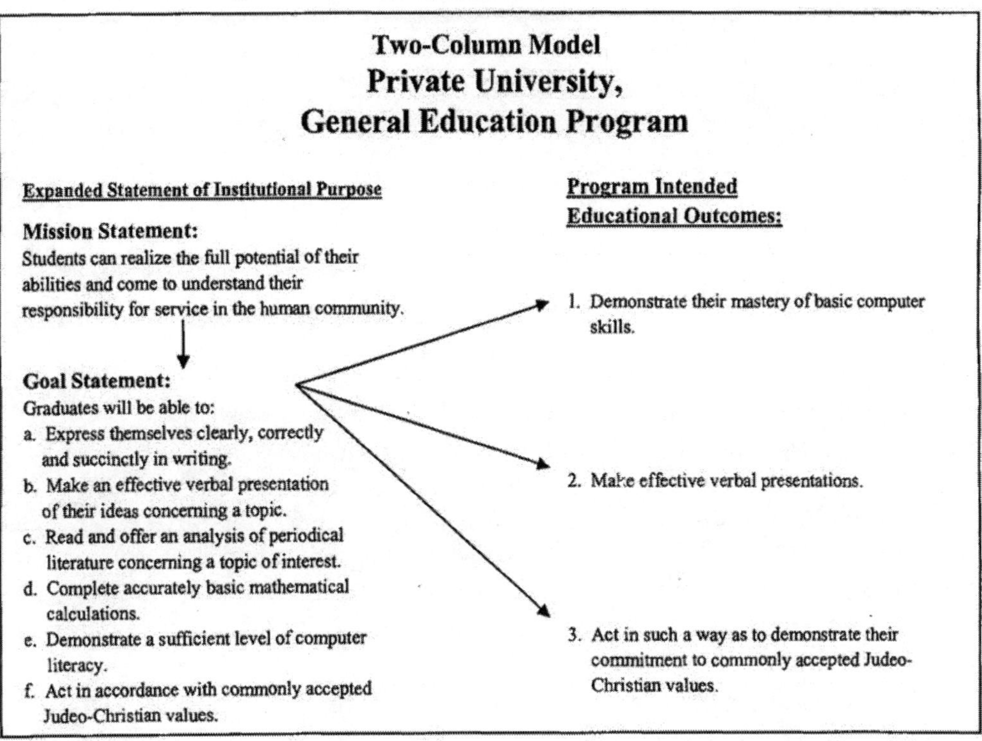

Formulation of the intended educational outcomes is *the* key first step in determining the appropriate means for assessment for the general education program. Cognitive, attitudinal and behavioral performance measures common on college and university campuses are next described.

CHAPTER IV

MEANS OF ASSESSMENT IN GENERAL EDUCATION

The general education intended educational outcomes described in Chapter III should lead logically to identification of the types of assessment to be conducted concerning each outcome. If you find that you have not identified intended educational outcomes for the general education program before reading this chapter, please return to Chapter III and work with the institution to identify educational (student) outcomes for your general education program. Otherwise, your institution may spend a good bit of unnecessary and wasted time, effort, and expense in assessment of general education.

As is the case concerning assessment in the major, there are both quantitative and qualitative types of assessment conducted concerning general education. However, in the case of general education, little qualitative type of assessment is conducted on most campuses, thereby leaving the bulk of assessment in the subject of general education to be quantitative in nature.

Qualitative Means of Assessment

Qualitative assessment can be described as those assessment activities culminating in an informed judgement as opposed to a specific quantitative score. The type of qualitative assessment in general education most likely to be implemented is that concerning written communication. On a number of campuses, portfolios of student writing samples have been collected and ultimately reviewed as to their accomplishment of the general education outcomes regarding written communication established by the institution. Portfolio assessment is a valid form of general education assessment.

Three suggestions are offered concerning portfolio assessment of general education written communication:

- First, establish at least a set of general rubrics which describe what the desired level of written communication competency should resemble.
- Compile the portfolios so that there is consistency between portfolios (e.g. they all contain the first paper from one class, the fourth project from another class, and the final examination from a third class).
- Determine in advance to what extent during a student's matriculation each work

included in the portfolio should exhibit the characteristics described in the rubrics established.

The above having been accomplished, it is possible to go about evaluating the extent of achievement of written communication outcomes.

It must be borne in mind, however, that portfolio assessment is among the most time consuming and expensive (in terms of faculty time) means of assessment available in higher education. The authors are personally aware of one institution having a considerable space dedicated to the storage of portfolios and a half-time employee identified as the "curator of portfolios." A number of institutions have begun portfolio assessment of writing only to find it so labor intensive that they have been unable to sustain it even through the first iteration of the project. Institutions should take great care before committing large amounts of faculty time to this type of valid assessment effort.

Quantitative Means of Assessment

The types of quantitative assessment normally described in the literature include assessment of cognitive student achievement or learning, the attitudes of students or graduates toward the institution and their program, and their performance or behavior upon completion of the general education program. Quantitative assessment can be described as that assessment resulting in a specific numeric score.

Cognitive Means of Assessment

Cognitive assessment in general education includes absolute measures of learning or academic achievement as well as measures of growth in these abilities from the time students entered the institution. In most cases, cognitive achievement in general education is measured at the end of the second year by which time students are assumed to have taken most of their general education program courses. While some students will delay certain courses until later in their academic career, others will have taken excessive amounts in those fields in which courses are required by the end of their sophomore year. Since assessment of the general education program deals with group data these phenomena tend to "wash out" as long as only group data are being considered.

Institutions must choose either locally developed or standardized means of cognitive assessment in general education. The advantages of the use of standardized means of assessment in general education include those shown in Figure 17. Of these advantages, probably the ready availability of instrumentation is among the most frequently cited by institutions as the reason for selecting to use a standardized test in assessment of general education. This is often the case because of the institution's delay in beginning assessment activities in this area which results in an urgent need to "get some assessment done."

The disadvantages of using standardized tests in assessment of general education are depicted in Figure 18. Most of these disadvantages can be cited regarding any

Figure 17

Advantages of Utilizing Standardized Tests in Assessment of General Education

- Ability to Make Normative Comparisons

- Ready Availability of Instruments

- Comprehensive Coverage of Subject

- Acceptance of Validity of Results by Those Outside the Institution

---

Figure 18

Disadvantages of Utilizing Standardized Tests in Assessment of General Education

- Fit with Campus General Education Outcomes
- Open Hostility of Faculty Toward Standardized Testing in Some Liberal Arts Fields

- Unwillingness of Faculty to Use Results

- Cost

---

standardized testing in higher education. However, the often open hostility of faculty toward standardized testing in general education is clearly noteworthy. This is partially attributable to the fact that a large number of the disciplines contributing to general education (humanities, fine arts, etc.) are either philosophically opposed to standardized testing or highly suspect of standardized testing based upon professional judgment or research in their fields. This cynicism is fueled by the use of standardized tests with multiple choice items that claim to measure a student's ability to write.

Standardized testing regarding general education is divided into comprehensive tests covering the broad field of general education and more specialized instruments testing a single aspect of general education such as critical thinking. The ACT Collegiate Assessment of Academic Proficiency (CAAP), ETS Academic Profile, and the College Basic Academic Subjects Examination (CBASE) from the University of Missouri are the most often identified comprehensive measures of general education cognitive performance. These tests are designed for administration at the end of students' second year of study; however, they can also be administered at the close of the baccalaureate program. Normative data for this latter administration must be carefully considered in order that one group's accomplishments in general education after two years are not compared with another group's after four years.

ACT Collegiate Assessment of Academic Proficiency (CAAP)
The CAAP test consists of five 40-minute modules plus an optional writing sample. Each module can be administered separately. The writing, reading, mathematics, critical thinking, and science reasoning content areas of the CAAP parallel the enhanced ACT Assessment Test utilized by many institutions as an entrance examination. Several of these modules also directly relate to the ACT ASSET and COMPAS examinations utilized as placement tests on many campuses. The contents of the CAAP modules are described in Figure 19.

Figure 19

Summary of the Contents of the Collegiate Assessment of Academic Proficiency (CAAP) Test

- **Writing Skills Test**: Measures students' comprehension of punctuation, grammar, sentence structure, and other elements necessary for effective written English.

- **Reading Test**: Measures reading comprehension by requiring examinees to refer to explicit statements and then reason, draw conclusions, and generalize beyond the written material.

- **Mathematics Test**: Measures mathematical skills in content areas ranging from pre-algebra to introductory calculus.

- **Critical Thinking Test**: Measures students' skills in classifying and analyzing the elements of an argument, and in evaluating and extending an argument.

- **Science Reasoning Test**: Measures scientific reasoning skills, but does not emphasize factual knowledge. Students are required to interpret graphs, tables, and scatter plots, analyze experimental results, and compare alternative hypotheses or viewpoints.

- **Writing (Essay) Test**: Measures students' skills in formulating and supporting assertions about a given issue, and in organizing and connecting major ideas.

Studies of students at two-year and four-year colleges found low to moderate correlation between CAAP scores and end of sophomore year grades (0.34–0.38) and also discovered that CAAP scores have moderately predictive validity for grades during the junior year. In addition, research indicates that average CAAP scores increase from the freshman year to the end of the sophomore year indicating the knowledge or skills gained through courses taken.

Of particular interest to institutions using the ACT Assessment Test as an entrance examination or the ASSET or COMPAS tests as placement examinations, will be the statistical relationship developed between those measures and the CAAP scores two years later. Using this procedure, ACT can estimate CAAP scores two years later (based upon national normative data) of groups of entering students using the ACT input (entrance) measures such as the ACT Assessment Tests or their diagnostic tests utilized for placement, ASSET or COMPAS. This is the only standardized comprehensive general test which readily facilitates measurement of growth during the first two years of higher education by establishing this pre- vs. post-test comparison.

The CAAP is frequently chosen by two-year institutions as a means for general education assessment. Note that the scales covered on the CAAP are primarily related to the basic skills outlined earlier in Chapter III with very limited coverage of the higher order thinking skills identified in that chapter. Little if any coverage is provided concerning the "value development level" of learning in general education (see page 28). ACT specifically states that the CAAP *does not measure content knowledge* in the area identified, but the ability to utilize basic skills in these fields.

Further information concerning the CAAP test is available from:
ACT National Office
2201 North Dodge Street
P.O. Box 168
Iowa City, IA 52243-0168
Telephone: 319-337-1000
Fax: 319-339-3021

Educational Testing Service (ETS) Academic Profile
Of the three instruments described, Academic Profile is the oldest. Content validity was ensured during instrument development by working with faculty to address the concerns expressed in the Association of American Colleges 1985 report "Integrity in the College Curriculum." Academic Profile was originally designed as a norm referenced examination only with a total score and seven subscores (also norm referenced). Subsequently, criterion reference subscores were provided in the skill dimensions area. A brief description of ETS Academic Profile is contained in Figure 20.

Though the academic content areas of Academic Profile relate to humanities, social sciences and natural sciences, it is important to note that they do not claim to provide measures of the extent of knowledge of students in these areas. The areas are utilized as a background against which students' skills in reading, writing, use of mathematical data and critical thinking are tested.

Academic Profile was under redevelopment during academic year 1999-2000 and a revised and refined instrument is expected on the market within the year. Information concerning Academic Profile may be obtained from:

Figure 20

Summary of the Academic Content Areas and Skill Dimensions of the ETS Academic Profile

<u>Academic Content Areas</u>

Humanities:
Within subjects related to humanities, tests students'
ability to read carefully, etc., and does not measure
students' knowledge in humanities.

Social Sciences:
Within subjects related to introductory social science
classes, tests students' ability to think critically, etc.,
but does not measure students' knowledge of social
sciences.

Natural Sciences:
Within themes and ideas related to introductory natural
science classes, tests students' ability to make
judgments about argumentation, etc.; however, is not a
measure of natural science knowledge.

<u>Skill Dimensions</u>

**College level reading/critical
thinking:**
norm-referenced and criterion
referenced sub-scores provided

College level writing:
norm-referenced and criterion
referenced sub-scores provided

Using mathematical data:
norm-referenced and criterion
referenced sub-scores provided

Figure 21

Summary of the College BASE Subject Area and Reasoning Competencies

<u>Subject Area</u>

English Clusters:
   -Reading and Literature (reading comprehension
    and knowledge of major literacy works)
   -Writing (pre-writing, composing, and revising)
Mathematics Clusters:
   -General Math (basic computational skills
    and statistical reasoning)
   -Algebra (college level algebra)
   -Geometry (concepts and ability to use these
    in calculations)
Science Clusters:
   -Laboratory/field (work applications of the
    scientific method)
   -Fundamental concepts (life, earth, and
    physical science)
Social Studies Cluster:
   -History (knowledge and causal relationships)
   -Social Science (geography, economics, and
    political science)

<u>Reasoning Competencies</u>

Interactive Reasoning:

Beginning to understand information
presented.

Strategic Reasoning:

Establishment of basis for inferences
and deductions.

Adaptive Reasoning:

Ability to synthesize new rules or
theories.

Higher Education Assessment Program
Educational Testing Service
Princeton, NJ 08541-0001
Telephone: 609-771-7076

College Basic Academic Subjects Examination
The College Basic Academic Subjects Examination (CBASE) is a criterion referenced achievement test that can be used to evaluate both individuals and programs
of general education. CBASE provides a composite score, four subject subscores,
and three reasoning scores as described in Figure 21.

Unlike the two earlier described instruments, CBASE measures specific knowledge and skills obtained in introductory level classes. It provides (in the authors'
opinion) the most useful set of subscores for curriculum improvement purposes and
institutional analysis of the three instruments described. However, the number of
institutions utilizing CBASE is substantially smaller than that of Academic Profile
or CAAP.

Information concerning CBASE may be obtained from:
Assessment Resource Center
University of Missouri-Columbia
2800 Maguire Boulevard
Columbia, MO 65201
Telephone: 800-366-8232

Assessment of Critical Thinking
Each of the instruments previously described (the ACT Collegiate Assessment of
Academic Proficiency), ETS Academic Profile and CBASE from the University of
Missouri) contains a slightly different set of critical thinking subscales. The advantage of using any of the subscales included in these more comprehensive instruments described in Figures 18-21 is that while gaining information concerning more
basic skills such as reading, writing, and math application, a measure of critical
thinking ability is forthcoming at no additional expense or time.

On the other hand, those institutions unwilling to accept one of the critical thinking subscales contained in the comprehensive general education instruments
described in Figures 18-21 may wish to consider a separate instrument such as those
shown in Figure 22. The Watson-Glaser Critical Thinking Appraisal (CTA) is typical of standardized objective tests of critical thinking ability. It is an objective measure which has been used extensively since the mid-1960s. The CTA provides five
subscores including: inference, recognition of assumptions, deduction, interpreta-
tion, and evaluation of arguments, as well as a total score for each individual taking
the examination. Some researchers have questioned the extent to which the CTA is
sensitive to educational effects.

The California Critical Thinking Skills Test (CCTST) includes five skills: inter-
pretation, analysis, evaluation, inference, and explanation. While the CCTST does
seem to be sensitive to the educational effects of courses specifically designed to

enhance the critical thinking skills in the test, there remain several questions concerning the influence of reading level on the examination.

Figure 22

Standardized Test of Critical Thinking

- The Watson-Glaser Critical Thinking Appraisal (CTA)

- The California Critical Thinking Skills Test (CCTST)

- Tasks in Critical Thinking

The Tasks in Critical Thinking test was developed jointly by the Educational Testing Service and the College Board. It differs from the previously described separate tests of critical thinking in that it is performance based, rather than being the typical multiple choice recognition type of items, and it provides a group score rather than individual scores. The Task is set around a number of generalized tasks in the humanities, social sciences and natural sciences. Students are challenged to solve a particular dilemma or task, and their ability to do so is recorded based upon a group of standardized rubrics. The skill areas measured by Task are inquiry, analysis, and communications. Within each of these separate scales, subscales are identified and measured. The Task clearly represents a departure from the standardized multiple choice type of format.

Reviews of these instruments by Dr. Gary Pike are contained in his column *Assessment Measures* in Volume 8, Number 4, Volume 9, Number 2, and Volume 11, Number 6 of the Assessment Update newsletter published by Jossey-Bass. These reviews have been one of the bases for the psychometric analysis of the test cited in this section.

Issues in Standardized General Education Assessment
The issues reflected in Figure 23 are only the most apparent regarding standardized assessment in general education. While a standardized test such as the licensure examination in Nursing may be assumed to reflect mastery of a commonly accepted body of knowledge, standardized tests are even more suspect by many faculty in areas covered by general education where there is considerably less agreement.

Figure 23

Issues in <u>Standardized</u> General Education Assessment

- Match of Test to Outcomes and Curriculum

- Importance of Subscales

- Normative Comparisons

- Standardized Assessment of Writing

- Student Motivation

Beyond much doubt, practitioners who have dealt with this subject identify the main issue in standardized assessment of general education as the match of the test items to the intended outcomes or curriculum through which students have matriculated at the institution. To begin with, the authors know of no incidence in which a standardized general education means of assessment has been accepted by faculty as a good match. Usually groups of faculty find one or more of the scales on each instrument not to fit what they are intending to accomplish in that aspect of general education. The issue is whether the standardized means of general education assessment described are such a bad fit as to preclude their further consideration. If that judgement is made, then the faculty making the decision need to consider the challenges associated with locally developed means of general education assessment later reviewed.

Each of the standardized means of assessment described (CAAP, Academic Profile, CBASE) provides at least one total score regarding the extent of general education academic achievement. It is highly unlikely that this *total* score will be of any practical use in curriculum or learning improvement as it is too general to have any utility for this purpose. Those considering use of these standardized means of assessment for general education need to pay particular attention to the scale and subscale scores provided by each instrument (often at several levels of specificity). These subscale scores are much more likely to pique faculty interest and lead to utilization of results for program improvement. It is these scale and subscale scores which will be most closely related to individual outcomes, rather than the total score for any of the general education assessment means described.

Many institutions seek to use standardized means of general education assessment to make normative comparisons of their students' accomplishments with those of students at other institutions. It would be entirely inappropriate for open admission institutions to compare their students' accomplishments with those of students at highly selective institutions. Frankly, there are those institutions whose students (because of the nature of their selective admission) will, as a group, score higher on standardized general education measures *at the time of their admission* than other institutions' students will score *after two years of collegiate general education.* Great care should be utilized in selection of the institution's peer group for such comparative purposes.

The ability to assess students' writing ability through a standardized objective test will never be accepted by faculty teaching writing or employed in an English department. Nonetheless, each of the instruments reviewed utilizes standardized items in a multiple choice format to provide some type of score concerning the participants ability to write. To their credit, the instruments reviewed also provide an option (at extra cost) for the institution to submit writing samples, which are then holistically scored by the individual testing services. However, before having actual writing samples reviewed by these standardized testing firms, institutions should ask themselves the question: "How will an overall or holistic writing score provide information through which to improve the writing program at our institution?" Often locally conducted or contracted analysis of writing samples will provide more useful results for program or learning improvement.

Student motivation is another major consideration for institutions utilizing standardized means for assessment of general education. Institutions can require through notification in their catalog that students take part in standardized (or for that matter any) means of assessment as part of their matriculation through the institution. They can not require that students *seriously* take part in any means of assessment. While some institutions require certain scores on standardized means of general education assessment before allowing their students to continue toward their degree, the authors do not recommend such a course of action unless the institution has excellent, readily available, and reasonably priced legal representation. The standardized instruments described previously are, in the authors' opinion, simply not sufficiently developed nor precise enough to provide individual scores upon which to base life-changing decisions such as continuation of a student on to a four-year degree.

If a specific score on one of the standardized general education measures described earlier is not required, how can institutions go about motivating students to be serious about completing the instruments which take roughly three hours? Institutions taking part in *Assessment Case Studies* (Agathon Press, 1995), determined that the best means for motivating a student to take part seriously in any type of assessment activity was to embed it in a course which the student was taking. The means of assessment can be used once for grading purposes in the class (and at least a small portion of the overall grade should be attributed to the means of assessment in order to motivate students) and subsequently reconsidered later and more broadly as a measure of general education by a panel of faculty. The primary problem with standardized testing in this approach to motivation in general education is the selection of classes normally taken at the close of the sophomore year or beginning of the junior year. Because of the flexibility in scheduling allowed students in selection of their courses, it is virtually impossible to use a single standardized means of assessment embedded in all sections of one class across the institution. The authors suggest that the institution select a representative group of classes, which most rising juniors take, and then embed the examination in a number of those course sections. This should result in a representative (though certainly not random) sample of students at approximately the close of the sophomore year or beginning of the junior year. This procedure is perhaps particularly important at two-year colleges where the motivational challenge is the most difficult. Because students transfer immediately after having taken the rising junior examination, the two-year college is not in a position to exert much leverage to entice students to take an examination seriously.

In those cases in which general education measures can't be embedded within courses, other means must be found through which to motivate students. Each campus needs to ask itself: "What makes students tick on our campus?" At one campus, competition between fraternities and sororities for the award of a highly visible trophy was utilized to motivate individual members of these organizations to contribute their time and energy to taking seriously an examination not otherwise required. On another campus, the registration system was modified to allow students scoring highest on the general education assessment measure to register first during their junior and senior year of attendance. While on still another campus, those students scoring particularly well on the general education means of assessment are awarded honors degrees with a seal affixed to their degree indicating the students' overall high level of achievement regarding general education.

Perhaps the most interesting means of student motivation the authors are aware of was initiated by an urban four-year institution that had a parking problem. The institution established an "honors parking lot" in the middle of campus. Those students scoring well on the general education means of assessment were assured of parking in these spaces during their junior and senior years at the institution. The only problem encountered with this motivational approach was the deluge of faculty desiring to take the examination!

If state government or a system administration requires a standardized general education assessment measure such as those described (and a number do), then student motivation becomes even more important. The fact that each student is required to take the examination by the state *will not* motivate the students to take the exam seriously unless their degree is withheld for a low score. Institutions need to consider the motivational techniques described above, as well as any others, to stimulate their students' performance on such a state-required examination. Under these circumstances, the scores of the students at each institution in the state will ultimately be published (often on the front page of most prominent state newspaper) to the great embarrassment of institutions who did not motivate their students sufficiently.

These issues and many more should be brought forward on the campus during discussions considering using standardized measures in the assessment of general education. Nonetheless, we make the following pertinent recommendations:

- It is suggested that the respective vendors be contacted and that the CAAP, CBASE, and Academic Profile examinations be brought onto the campus for review by the faculty.
- Each general education standardized means of assessment should be compared with the previously identified outcomes for general education. If this accomplishes nothing more than to bring discussions of general education down to earth from the glowing generalizations frequently associated therewith, then the time of those reviewing the examinations will have been well spent.
- The campus should then choose whichever means of standardized general education assessment seems to fit its existing outcomes and curriculum best and conduct a pilot test of that instrument on a portion of the institution's rising juniors. Such a pilot test is advised to identify both logistical and substantive problems in such an administration before the much larger scale implementation to be accomplished is next considered. This activity is certain to both inform and inflame the discussions that are bound to take place after the results of this pilot administration are distributed.

Locally Developed Cognitive Means of Assessment in General Education
Locally developed means of cognitive assessment in general education exhibit the advantages and disadvantages shown in Figures 24 and 25. Perhaps the greatest advantage of locally developed means of cognitive assessment in general education is the ability to mold or shape these means in such a manner that they match the outcomes and curriculum of the institution. Acceptance by the faculty of this match goes a long way toward building their confidence in the results of these assessment activities and subsequent use of these results to improve general education programming. On the other hand, one should not underestimate the amount of work necessary to put in place locally developed means of assessment of general education. This burden has been sufficient in many (if not most) cases to limit assessment activities developed locally to "basic skills" such as the analysis of a writing sample and perhaps some type of test of the ability of students to do mathematical calculations.

It is important for faculty to understand that locally developed (or for that matter any) assessment in general education, is designed to take place beyond the course level. The implications of this statement are substantial as they preclude individual course grades awarded by an instructor from being utilized as a means of assessment. Whenever the individual instructor providing the instructional service is the sole evaluator of student academic achievement, the reliability of the assessment is subject to challenge. While faculty members will continue to grade individual students, in order to increase objectivity, assessment of the general education program has increasingly become a corporate responsibility of faculty at the departmental level. Hence, in order for means of assessment taking place within a course (i.e.

Figure 24

<u>Locally Developed</u> Cognitive Means of Assessment in General Education

Advantages:

- Readily Accepted by Regional Accreditors

- Ability to Design to "Fit" Institutional Outcomes and Curriculum

- More Ready Acceptance by Faculty Leading to Greater Likelihood of Use of Results

Figure 25

<u>Locally Developed</u> Cognitive Means of Assessment in General Education

Disadvantages:

- Time and Effort of Faculty to Construct, Maintain, and Administer

- Usually Limited in Scope to Writing and Math

- Little External Credibility

imbedded) to be used, the results of this assessment will need to be reviewed a second time by a panel of faculty broadly representative of those teaching in the discipline or department. This injunction does not preclude faculty at two-year colleges from utilizing grades awarded by four-year college faculty in follow-on courses as a means of assessment.

Figure 26

Relationship Between Individual Student Grading and Educational Outcomes Assessment

Individual Students Scored by Various Faculty

Criteria	Student 1	Student 2	Student 3	Student 4	Student 5	Criteria/Intended Educational Outcomes Average
Spelling	3	4	1	2	3	2.6
Grammar	2	5	3	2	5	3.4
Punctuation	4	5	2	3	4	3.6
Structure	4	3	4	5	3	3.8
TOTAL	13	17	10	12	15	
Individual Student Grade	C	A	D	C	B	

Analyze "Down the Columns" for Individual Student Grading
Analyze "Across the Rows" for Assessment of Intended Educational Outcomes Accomplishment

One technique which may help in working with faculty displeased with their inability to use their own course grades as a means of assessment is illustrated in Figure 26. This illustration, known as the "column and row model," depicts a situation common in general education in which faculty have agreed upon certain criteria through which to award grades such as those for written communication shown. These criteria are depicted in the row headings on the left side of Figure 26. Repeatedly, faculty evaluate individual students "down the column" as shown in this model to arrive at a course grade. While it is inappropriate to use the course grades reflected in the bottom row of this illustration as a means of assessment, program faculty can average across the rows to arrive at a specific finding regarding individual criteria such as Spelling. The means of assessment would indicate that graduates will be able to spell at an average of 3.0 on a 5.0 scale as reflected on the writing sample to which this criteria is applied. The resulting score of 2.6 in the example would provide guidance for program improvement. This enables the faculty to move relatively quickly from commonly agreed upon grading criteria to useful means of assessment without the specification of course grades as the means of assessment.

It is very rare (the authors know of only one institution among the over 200 with whom they have worked) that an institution prepares a locally developed comprehensive cognitive examination regarding general education. However, two other locally developed approaches to comprehensive cognitive assessment show some promise.

On some campuses faculty in the different disciplines servicing general education have agreed to administer either completely or partially common course examinations for all sections through which students completing general education pass. These examinations are administered and analyzed by the group of faculty in each department. This analysis is then combined with similar analyses from other departments resulting in a "cumulative" or comprehensive cognitive examination composed of the components contributed by each discipline.

Several other institutions have taken the approach of carefully selecting texts for their general education courses. Those texts selected all contain publisher-provided cognitive examinations based upon the material covered in the text. These examinations are administered and the results combined from across several disciplines to again result in a cumulative or comprehensive locally designed cognitive examination in general education. The obvious advantage of this approach is the ability to compare individual discipline responses at the institution with the criteria established in the textbook. The primary disadvantage of this approach is the limitation of assessment to the material presented in the textbooks.

General education cognitive assessment is among the most daunting challenges on college and university campuses. There clearly is no one "correct" means of assessment and most colleges field a mix of standardized and locally developed methods. The key in selection of those methods is to focus upon the means of assessment which are responsive to the outcomes stated and will result in data that faculty are likely to use for program improvement.

Attitudinize Means of Assessment in General Education
Attitudinal information drawn from questionnaires or surveys completed by students (a) while they are enrolled at the institution, (b) as they are leaving or (c) later as alumni of the institution, as well as surveys of employers, are frequently used in general education assessment (see Figure 27).

From these types of surveys, both respondents' opinions and reports of activities since leaving the institution may be gained. The opinions reflected or attitudes of students increase in value as the respondents to the means of assessment mature progressively from enrolled students to students at the time of graduation through their opinions as alumni. These opinions concerning institutional programs (including general education) remain relatively stable from the point of graduation to three to five years later. It has been the authors' experience, based on more than twenty thousand graduating student surveys and five thousand plus alumni survey responses at the University of Mississippi, that if students rate highly a particular program of instruction at the time of their graduation, they continue that level of appreciation later as alumni. On the other hand, if students felt ill served by a program when they graduated, their alumni responses continue to reflect that opinion three to five years later. There is no evidence to sustain the often stated position that students may not understand why they are being asked to go through certain instructional processes now, but will appreciate those processes and the resultant learning at a later time.

Figure 27

Occasions for Attitudinal Assessment in General Education

- Students While Enrolled

- Students at the Time of Graduation

- Alumni Once They Have Left the Institution

- Employers of Graduates

The other type of information, which can be gained from surveys of alumni, relates to reports of events which have taken place either at the time of the completion of the program or since their departure from the institution. Graduating student surveys frequently ask questions about admission to graduate school and job placement. Alumni surveys often seek information about graduate school completion, employment, participation in continuing professional education, licensure, reading habits, church attendance patterns, etc. In many cases, institutions will need to infer, from activities reported by alumni, the acquisition of certain values intended by the institution during the alumni's matriculation on the campus.

Employer surveys represent a special and very important type of attitudinal assessment. In this case, it is the attitude of employers toward their employees' (the institution's graduates) ability to perform on the job. In many cases, this includes the skills and abilities such as writing and oral communication commonly gained through general education. Those coordinating assessment in general education need to work closely with the various departments conducting assessment in the students' majors to ensure that feedback gained concerning general educational from employer surveys is focused on the educational outcomes identified for the general education program.

There are distinct limitations to attitudinal assessment. The most obvious of these limitations is the response rate to many questionnaires. Surveys of students while they are enrolled at an institution (without heavy-handed methods to coerce responses) frequently result in well less than 50 percent response rates. In most cases, questionnaires placed in the mail to students at the time of graduation or later as alumni will probably struggle to reach between a 20 and 30 percent response rate. However, response rates in excess of 95 percent can be realized by placing the graduating student questionnaire in the out-processing stream for students at the time of graduation. For this reason, the authors suggest implementation at the earliest time possible of a graduating student survey covering a number of subjects, from satisfaction with general education as well as the student's major to educational support and administrative services.

A less obvious limitation regarding attitudinal assessment is the fleeting acceptance of such assessment as primary evidence of student academic achievement by some of the regional accrediting associations. Earlier in the assessment movement, attitudinal assessment (which is relatively easier to accomplish than other means of assessment) was extensively utilized as primary evidence regarding the accomplishment of many intended educational (student) outcomes. This practice, which in the authors' "Southern speak," might be described as an "attaboy," was constituted in most cases by a simple attitudinal affirmation on the part of the student or graduate that they had learned or acquired a skill while in attendance at the institution. Such means of assessment over the last two to three years have been eschewed by most of the regional accrediting agencies as primary evidence of student achievement. They are, in fact, described as "indirect measures" or perceptions on the part of the student or alumni rather than more direct measures such as cognitive, behavioral, or performance assessment. While these attitudinal means of assessment remain accepted, they are now viewed as supporting information regarding the subject. Any instance in which only attitudinal means of assessment are provided should be viewed with great skepticism regarding acceptance by any regional accrediting association.

Standardized Surveys Regarding General Education
Attitudinal assessment regarding general education may be implemented through locally designed instruments or utilizing nationally standardized surveys. These two sources of attitudinal assessment offer rather distinct strengths and limitations (see Figure 28).

Nationally standardized surveys have the advantages of ready availability and normative data for comparison purposes. American College Testing (ACT), the College Board in conjunction with the National Center for Higher Education Management Systems, and the College Student Experiences Questionnaire (CSEQ) from Indiana University, provide excellent means for standardized feedback regarding students' general education experiences (see Figure 29). Each of these vendors will provide, on very short notice, well designed instruments, suggestions for their distribution, and standardized reports regarding student perceptions of their academic accomplishments. For an additional cost, most of these vendors will also (a) provide custom processing of the results as dictated by the institution and/or, (b) actually prepare and mail the survey and process and distribute the results of the survey.

Figure 28

<u>Standardized Surveys</u> in Assessment of General Education

<u>Strengths</u>

Ready Availability

Normative Comparisons

Ability to Add Locally Developed Items

<u>Limitations</u>

Match of Survey Items with Actual Campus Outcomes

Cost

Lack of Campus "Identity"

Figure 29

Sources and Examples of Standardized Attitudinal Surveys Related to Assessment of General Education

- American College Testing Evaluation Survey Services - *College Outcomes Survey*

- College Board and National Center for Higher Education Management Systems - *Program Completer and Graduating Student Questionnaire*

- Indiana University, Center for Post-Secondary Research and Planning - *College Student Experiences Questionnaire (CSEQ)*

On the other hand, nationally standardized surveys exhibit some clear limitations. Because general education outcomes are anything but standardized from campus to campus, the match of items on these surveys with actual campus intended educational outcomes is frequently imprecise at best. Second, it is highly unlikely that these standardized instruments will cover *all* of the general education outcomes on which institutions desire student feedback. Finally, nationally standardized surveys or questionnaires are also more expensive in terms of out-of-pocket cost than locally developed surveys. Their cost ranges from several dollars per instrument to considerably more based upon the number of surveys, the specific services required by the campus, and other factors. Finally, standardized surveys generally lack institutional identification in their appearance.

Nationally standardized surveys are frequently chosen by relatively small institutions, which often lack the necessary staff support services to construct their own instruments. Standardized surveys are also chosen by institutions feeling a particularly urgent need to "get some assessment data." Such institutions can move from this realization to the receipt of nationally standardized survey results within a matter of months, though at a considerable price.

A brief description of each of the most frequently utilized nationally standardized attitudinal survey instruments referenced above is contained in Appendix B of this publication. Information concerning the national source for further information and material concerning each survey is also provided.

Figure 30

<u>Locally Developed</u> Surveys in Attitudinal Assessment of General Education

<u>Strengths</u>

Specific Wording Related to Institutional Outcomes

Ability to Adjust Items

Institutional Identification

<u>Limitations</u>

Effort to Produce

No Normative Comparisons Possible

Locally Developed Means of Attitudinal Assessment Regarding General Education
The alternative to the use of nationally standardized surveys for assessment in general education is the production of such surveys by the institution. This choice is more commonly exercised at larger institutions employing sufficient staff to produce quality survey instruments. These locally developed instruments represent the institution and should convey an image of professionalism.

Locally developed attitudinal surveys have a number of strengths and limitations (see Figure 30). Among the strengths of locally developed surveys are the following. First, the items concerning general education can be tailored exactly to match the intended general education outcomes of the institution. There is no doubt that the results of the survey link directly to the institution's general education outcomes. Second, there exists the ability to readily adjust the items regarding general education as the focus of assessment of that program shifts. Finally, these questionnaires or surveys can be attractively printed and a public relations or identity value to the institution realized. An example of such is shown in Figure 31 which is printed in red and blue (the school colors) with the CEO's signature. Note that items 17, 19, 22, and 23 directly relate to the general education program of the institution and that the results of these items can be readily used for assessment purposes.

The single greatest disadvantage of locally developed attitudinal surveys is their relative labor intensiveness and the amount of time necessary to prepare quality surveys. Most locally developed attitudinal surveys take between six months and a year to design, layout, distribute, and prepare the programming necessary for report processing. This effort can easily occupy much of the time of one staff member for the period, and for the institution seeking to move quickly to acquire assessment data, this is not a viable course of action. On the other hand, once these locally developed instruments are designed and ready for processing, the out-of-pocket or per unit cost and time needed for conducting such locally developed surveys diminishes.

The choice of locally developed or standardized attitudinal surveys is certainly one which must be made by each institution depending on its circumstances. However, institutions must bear in mind that either type of survey provides students' opinions or perceptions of their education which are progressively a less valued means of assessment concerning the quality of general education programming. Such "indirect" evidence remains of some utility as a supporting piece of evidence, but should not be the primary piece of information provided upon which to judge the general education program's achievements.

Performance Assessment in General Education
Performance assessment takes place when a situation is contrived requiring the student to demonstrate a skill or value identified in general education outcomes while the student remains enrolled at the institution. Examples of performance assessment

Figure 31

Mark Reflex® by NCS EM-161209-2:63432   ED06   Printed in U.S.A.

THE UNIVERSITY OF MISSISSIPPI
GRADUATING STUDENT SURVEY

OFFICE USE ONLY

CONGRATULATIONS UPON COMPLETION OF YOUR DEGREE REQUIREMENTS AT OLE MISS! As an alumna or alumnus of our institution, I know that you take pride in your accomplishment and want to help further improve the educational experiences enjoyed by those who follow you at Ole Miss. To gather information concerning your Ole Miss experience, this brief questionnaire is provided for your completion. It asks for information about yourself and your plans after graduation, as well as the extent to which you are satisfied with Ole Miss in general, University services, and your specific degree program. Your answers will remain confidential and will be used to improve your alma mater's academic programs and administrative services. Please return this questionnaire when you file your Application for Diploma in the Office of the Registrar.

DEGREE PROGRAM CODE

USE NO. 2 PENCIL ONLY

CORRECT MARK   INCORRECT MARKS

Robert C. Khayat
Robert C. Khayat, Chancellor

BIOGRAPHICAL/ENROLLMENT DATA Indicate only one response for each item by marking the appropriate circle.

1. GENDER
- Male
- Female

2. RACE
- White
- Black
- Other

3. CITIZENSHIP
- U.S.
- Other

4. RESIDENCY AT TIME OF ADMISSION
- Resident of Mississippi
- Non-resident of Mississippi

5. CURRENT AGE
- 22 or under
- 23–25
- 26–28
- 29–31
- 32–34
- 35 or older

6. CURRENT STATUS
- Undergraduate
- Graduate

7A. (UNDERGRADUATE STUDENTS ONLY) WHILE PURSUING THIS DEGREE, DID YOU:
- Originally enroll (and remain) at Ole Miss
- Transfer from a 2-year institution
- Transfer from a 4-year institution

11. ARE YOU ACTIVE IN AN OLE MISS SOCIAL FRATERNITY OR SORORITY?
- Yes
- No

7B. (GRADUATE & LAW STUDENTS ONLY) UNDERGRADUATE DEGREE FROM:
- Ole Miss
- Other institution

8. NUMBER OF YEARS IN ATTENDANCE AT OLE MISS
- One
- Two
- Three
- Four
- Five
- Six+

9. PLEASE ESTIMATE YOUR CUMULATIVE GPA (including only Ole Miss courses) UPON COMPLETION OF THIS DEGREE.
- 3.75+
- 3.50–3.74
- 3.25–3.49
- 3.00–3.24
- 2.75–2.99
- 2.50–2.74
- 2.25–2.49
- 2.00–2.24
- Below 2.00

10. NUMBER OF SEMESTERS YOU HAVE LIVED IN AN OLE MISS RESIDENCE HALL.
- None
- One
- Two
- Three
- Four
- Five+

12. AVERAGE NUMBER OF HOURS EMPLOYED (ON/OFF CAMPUS) PER WEEK DURING THE PAST YEAR
- None
- 1–10
- 11–20
- 21–30
- 31–40
- 40+

PLANS FOLLOWING GRADUATION Indicate only one response for each item by marking the appropriate circle.

13. What are your immediate employment plans?
- (a) I plan to continue working in the same job I had prior to completing this educational program.
- (b) I plan to work in a job I recently obtained.
- (c) I am currently looking for a job.
- (d) I do not plan to work outside the home.
- (e) I plan to continue my education before working.
- (f) I have not yet formulated my employment plans.

14. If you indicated in #13 that you currently have or will be starting a new job, to what extent is it related to your major or area of study at Ole Miss?
- (a) Directly related.
- (b) Somewhat related.
- (c) Not related.

Is the job in Mississippi?
- (a) Yes.
- (b) No.

15. Do you currently have plans for additional education?
- (a) No, not at this time.
- (b) Yes, I plan to reenroll at this institution.
- (c) Yes, I plan to enroll at another institution. *
- (d) Yes, I have been accepted for enrollment at another institution. *
- (e) I am currently undecided about additional education.

*If you chose responses "c" or "d" above, please indicate name of institution you will attend. →

16. If you indicated in #15 that you plan to continue your education, what is the highest degree you plan to earn?
- (a) Master's degree
- (b) Specialist degree (e.g., Ed.S.)
- (c) Professional degree (e.g., medicine, law, theology)
- (d) Doctoral degree (e.g., Ph.D., Ed.D., D.B.A.)

GENERAL LEVEL OF SATISFACTION WITH ATTENDANCE AT THE UNIVERSITY (Undergraduate Students Only)

For each of the following items which apply, please indicate the extent of your agreement with the statement as it describes your experience at Ole Miss.

Within my degree program or because of my experiences at Ole Miss, I:	NOT APPLICABLE	STRONGLY AGREE	AGREE	NEUTRAL	DISAGREE	STRONGLY DISAGREE
17. Acquired a basic knowledge in the liberal arts (humanities, social sciences, and natural sciences).	NA	SA	A	N	D	SD
18. Felt academically challenged.	NA	SA	A	N	D	SD
19. Developed the ability to write effectively.	NA	SA	A	N	D	SD
20. Felt adequately prepared for graduate study in my major field.	NA	SA	A	N	D	SD
21. Was prepared to assume the responsibilities of my chosen profession.	NA	SA	A	N	D	SD
22. Developed the ability to express myself effectively through speaking.	NA	SA	A	N	D	SD
23. Developed multicultural and global perspectives.	NA	SA	A	N	D	SD
24. Would recommend to others that they study within the same program at Ole Miss.	NA	SA	A	N	D	SD
25. Would recommend Ole Miss to prospective students.	NA	SA	A	N	D	SD

Figure 31-Page 2

OPINIONS CONCERNING UNIVERSITY ENVIRONMENT AND SERVICES (Graduate and Undergraduate Students)

Please indicate your level of satisfaction with each of the following University environmental conditions and services which you have used or directly experienced.

Environment and Services	NOT APPLICABLE OR DID NOT USE (NA)	VERY SATISFIED (VS)	SATISFIED (S)	NEUTRAL (N)	UN-SATISFIED (U)	VERY UN-SATISFIED (VU)
26. Admissions	NA	VS	S	N	U	VU
27. Telephone Registration	NA	VS	S	N	U	VU
28. Regular Registration	NA	VS	S	N	U	VU
29. Fee Payment Process	NA	VS	S	N	U	VU
30. Bursar Office Services	NA	VS	S	N	U	VU
31. Academic Advising in School or College	NA	VS	S	N	U	VU
32. University Counseling Center	NA	VS	S	N	U	VU
33. Teaching and Learning Center Services/Disability Services	NA	VS	S	N	U	VU
34. Recognition and Promotion of Cultural Diversity	NA	VS	S	N	U	VU
35. Student Housing and Residence Life Services and Programs	NA	VS	S	N	U	VU
36. Student Programming Board Programs and Activities	NA	VS	S	N	U	VU
37. Department of Campus Recreation	NA	VS	S	N	U	VU
38. International Student Advisory Services	NA	VS	S	N	U	VU
39. Dean of Students Office	NA	VS	S	N	U	VU
40. Student Media/Newspaper, Yearbook, Radio, and Television	NA	VS	S	N	U	VU
41. Financial Aid Processed in Timely Manner	NA	VS	S	N	U	VU
42. University Police Department Public Safety Services	NA	VS	S	N	U	VU
43. Student Health Service	NA	VS	S	N	U	VU
44. Student Health Education Presentations/Programs/Counseling	NA	VS	S	N	U	VU
45. Student Health Center Pharmacy	NA	VS	S	N	U	VU
46. Career Services Center Information	NA	VS	S	N	U	VU
47. Financial Aid Services	NA	VS	S	N	U	VU
48. Food Services	NA	VS	S	N	U	VU
49. Overall Classroom Conditions	NA	VS	S	N	U	VU
50. Condition and Maintenance of University Grounds	NA	VS	S	N	U	VU
51. J.D. Williams Library and its Music and Science Branch Libraries	NA	VS	S	N	U	VU
52. Law Library	NA	VS	S	N	U	VU
53. Computer Center Services	NA	VS	S	N	U	VU
54. Bookstore	NA	VS	S	N	U	VU
55. Graduate School Office	NA	VS	S	N	U	VU

ITEMS RELATED TO YOUR DEGREE PROGRAM

While the opinions you expressed above concerning the University in general are important, your thoughts about your specific degree program are most important. When you received this form, you were also provided a separate sheet of colored paper with items (numbered 56–75) that relate directly to your degree program. Please indicate below the extent of your agreement with each statement contained on the colored paper.

	NOT APPLICABLE	STRONGLY AGREE	AGREE	NEUTRAL	DISAGREE	STRONGLY DISAGREE			NOT APPLICABLE	STRONGLY AGREE	AGREE	NEUTRAL	DISAGREE	STRONGLY DISAGREE
56.	NA	SA	A	N	D	SD		66.	NA	SA	A	N	D	SD
57.	NA	SA	A	N	D	SD		67.	NA	SA	A	N	D	SD
58.	NA	SA	A	N	D	SD		68.	NA	SA	A	N	D	SD
59.	NA	SA	A	N	D	SD		69.	NA	SA	A	N	D	SD
60.	NA	SA	A	N	D	SD		70.	NA	SA	A	N	D	SD
61.	NA	SA	A	N	D	SD		71.	NA	SA	A	N	D	SD
62.	NA	SA	A	N	D	SD		72.	NA	SA	A	N	D	SD
63.	NA	SA	A	N	D	SD		73.	NA	SA	A	N	D	SD
64.	NA	SA	A	N	D	SD		74.	NA	SA	A	N	D	SD
65.	NA	SA	A	N	D	SD		75.	NA	SA	A	N	D	SD

COMMENTS

Please feel free to add your written comments in the space provided at the right and return this form to the Office of the Registrar at the time you file your Application for Diploma.

are indicated in Figure 32. There is no better vehicle for conducting assessment of verbal communications than the videotaping of student presentations and subsequent review of a sample of these tapes based upon commonly agreed to rubrics or a checklist. In many instances, institutions identify values such as ethics, globalism, commitment to cultural diversity, Judeo-Christian commitment, etc., which they expect students to take forward into their adult lives. An excellent means through which to assess the impact of the institution's general education program on students is to place students in a case study requiring them to demonstrate those values or skills while still in attendance at the institution. Finally, analysis of written prose is the most common type of performance assessment regarding writing. Students are not being tested for their knowledge of grammar or spelling, but rather their ability to actually write, using correct grammar and spelling.

Figure 32

Examples of <u>Performance</u> Assessment in General Education

- Video Tape of Oral Presentations

- Responses to Case Studies

- Analysis of Written Prose

The strength of performance or "authentic" assessment lies in the fact that it offers *direct evidence* of the students' abilities or values. There is no implication or inference that needs be drawn, and the tendency to report or demonstrate socially acceptable responses is minimized. However, performance assessment requires a considerable period of time and effort to logistically prepare and conduct. On balance, an institution should clearly consider at least a limited number of performance assessment measures regarding general education.

Behavioral Observation as a Means of Assessment in General Education
Behavioral observation type assessment takes place when the actions of students are observed or reported and these actions are linked to intended educational outcomes. However, in some cases in general education, the students' reported or observed actions either while in attendance or after leaving the institution must be assumed to *imply* a certain set of values. In most cases in the major, this linkage is very direct through reports of employment, admission to graduate school, etc. Examples of behavioral types of assessment in general education are shown in Figure 33.

Figure 33

Examples of Behavioral <u>Observation</u> in Assessment of General Education

- Voting in Student Elections

- Voluntary Attendance at Fine Arts Presentations

- Participation in Public Service Activities as Alumni

- Religious Service Attendance Patterns

If it is the institution's intention, as stated in its general education program educational (student) outcomes, that students become committed to taking part in the democratic process, then observation of voting patterns in student elections would seem like a logical behavioral indicator. If appreciation of the fine and performing arts represents a general education outcome listed by the institution, *voluntary* attendance at fine arts presentations by students would be one type of behavioral measure. Participation in public service activities as alumni could easily be an indicator or measure of the development of social consciousness as a part of general education. Finally, church attendance following graduation is an often cited behavioral measure of a commitment to Judeo-Christian beliefs.

Assessment of Values or Beliefs
The transmittal to future generations of various sets of values or beliefs has been among the hallmarks of general education in American colleges and universities. From its earliest inception, much of private or denominationally based education has been focused upon transmitting to new generations the values and beliefs of their forefathers. Other private institutions such as Harvard University have identified their students' commitment to the democratic process as essential. Many public institutions cite a sense of commitment to cultural diversity or development of a global perspective by their students as an important outcome of their general education program. It is precisely these value- or belief-oriented outcome statements that

directly contribute to assessment in general education being the most difficult type of assessment at any institution. It is not accidental that values development was cited in Chapter II as the highest form of educational outcome for an institution's general education program.

Private institutions are cautioned not to abandon such essential values or beliefs in their general education programs simply because they are difficult to assess. The existence of these values or beliefs are often at the core of private institutions' reason for being. To abandon these values in the face of assessment challenges clearly represents a misunderstood set of institutional priorities.

When beginning value- and/or belief-based assessment in higher education, an institution must identify whether it has committed to the *existence* of certain values or beliefs on the part of its graduates or to the *enhancement* or *change* of values and beliefs while students are enrolled in the general education program and other components of the institution. Commitment of the institution to changing values and beliefs requires both a pre- and a post-test in the research/assessment design. Ascertaining the existence of certain values or beliefs at the time of graduation or after two years in attendance as a rising junior is a formidable, but less daunting challenge, as it requires only a post-test in the research/assessment design. The nature of the design (existence or change) should be readily apparent from the intended outcome.

Figure 34

Means for Assessment of <u>Values or Beliefs</u> in General Education

- Asking Respondents

- Demonstration of Values Through Action

- Alumni Reporting Activities Indicative of Specified Values or Beliefs

---

There are three primary means of assessment regarding outcomes or values in general education: asking, demonstrating, and reporting (see Figure 34). If you ask a student or graduate if they are ethical, have certain Judeo-Christian beliefs, etc., there are very few respondents who will deny these values. The socially acceptable response will be offered on virtually every occasion. One of the more widespread instruments utilized to reflect student values is the Cooperative Institutional

Research Program (CIRP) annual questionnaire administered to entering freshmen and originated by the Higher Education Research Institute (HERI) at the University of California, Los Angeles (UCLA). This instrument originated by Dr. Sandy Astin and his colleagues, annually collects responses from tens of thousands of entering students across the United States regarding their needs, values and beliefs. These data are often quoted in the *Chronicle of Higher Education* in reference to surveys describing the political views of the students as ranging from conservative to liberal. Less well known is a companion survey to the CIRP which seeks to ascertain students beliefs or values at the time of their graduation. This survey is also available from HERI.

The Counsel for Christian Colleges and Universities (CCCU) collaborative assessment project entitled "Taking Values Seriously: Assessing the Mission of Church Related Higher Education," funded by the Fund for the Improvement of Post-secondary Education (FIPSE), is the best known example of a large scale and systematic approach to values assessment. The project originally hypothesized an increase in commitment of students to the values included in these institutions' general education programs. The data resulting from this six-year study indicate only a slight increase in the values orientation of CCCU students during their attendance at these colleges. On the other hand, this is a considerable accomplishment considering that other studies have fairly consistently reported significant declines in religious attitudes, values, and behaviors during the college years. To learn more about this collaborative assessment project and view specific examples of such values related assessment, contact the CCCU website at: www.cccu.org/news/assess.html.

Demonstrating a commitment to certain values or beliefs while enrolled at the institution is, in the authors' opinion, probably a more reliable measure of the existence of these values than is simply *asking* the students or graduates. This type of demonstration often takes place within case studies in which various solutions to a case study have been predetermined by the faculty to represent or not represent the religious, diversity, ethical or globalism values identified in the institution's educational (student) outcomes for general education. These case studies may take place in each program's major as part of a final capstone experience and their results refocused on the institution's general education program. In addition, there are behavioral patterns (participation in public service activities, campus religious organizations etc.) that may be assumed to reflect acquisition of the values identified. It is important that this participation be *voluntary* on the part of the students (as opposed to required for a course) if this activity is to indeed reflect their own acquisition of the value intended. It should be borne in mind that the acquisition of the value intended may *or may not* be caused by the institution's influence. It may well be the result place of other events or influences during or prior to college attendance.

The reporting by alumni of activities indicative of the acquisition of specific values or beliefs is the final common type of assessment regarding this subject. Implementation of this approach requires that the faculty identify which specific activities (church attendance patterns, participation in public service activities, reading habits, enrollment in continuing education, etc.) during a graduate's life would reflect acquisition of the value or belief intended as part of the institution's general education outcomes. Respondents to alumni surveys will, for the most part, accurately report whether they have taken part in these activities. The chief limitation to this approach (as noted earlier) is that adoption of these values or beliefs must be inferred from actions later in life that may or may not be the result of other variables. During the 1950s, higher education sought almost universally to educate students to "save for their retirement" as a result (at least partially) of experiences during the Great Depression. The current actual diminishing investments in traditional savings accounts would appear to reverse accomplishment of this intended outcome. However, in reality, this trend is more the result of low interest rates, the availability of alternative investments, and the reduction in the increase of discretionary funds available to many families more than to any desire not to save.

Each of these means of assessment for values or beliefs has its role to play in this important and difficult endeavor. If your institution is committed to the transmission of a set of values or beliefs, then the authors believe that it is essential that you begin the assessment process regarding these values or beliefs concurrently with the more concrete aspects of general education, but that the initial set of outcomes chosen for general education have no more than one such intended value or belief for assessment early in implementation. However, completely avoiding assessment of these value statements or beliefs not only is contrary to the institution's commitment to them, but invites questioning by regional accreditation visiting team members as to the reason(s) for such an obvious omission.

Establishment of the Criteria for Success Regarding General Education

The purpose of the assessment activities described in this chapter is not "to do assessment." The information resulting from the assessment activities conducted by an institution is the *means to the end* of our endeavor which is *improving the campus's general education program*. The single greatest mechanism through which a campus can stimulate this use of results is, in the authors' opinion, the creation of the Criteria for Success regarding each of the means of assessment identified.

The criterion for success identifies for each means of assessment how well students completing the general education program ought to perform if the program is functioning at an adequate level. This criterion for success (known on some campuses as a benchmark, target, etc.) is established by the faculty for their exclusive use. It is not a tool for making administrative judgments concerning the program, but for the faculty's use in determining the adequacy of program performance. The criteria for success should be set before assessment is done. This means that faculty, after establishing the means of assessment, need to make a judgment concerning what they would consider as adequate performance reflective of their program's functioning appropriately on this means of assessment.

The criteria for success (except in the case of value-related outcomes) should be based upon the academic preparation of the students enrolled as they enter the institution, the time or duration of the program, and other resource-related issues such as level of faculty staffing, physical facilities, equipment, etc. Whether the criteria for success appear to set an overly ambitious target or one easily attained makes little difference, since the faculty are setting it for their own use. Should the assessment data actually fall short of the criteria for success, faculty are welcome to reconsider the degree of reasonableness in their initial criteria for success and lower the expectations for the next iteration if they believe the criteria to have been mistakenly set. However, it is the authors' experience that in most cases, rather than lowering criteria that were thoughtfully established at the beginning, most faculty groups after a period of reflection will start to adjust the program to meet their original expectations. If the criteria are set at a modest level, faculty often raise the criteria in the next iteration. Faculty are urged not to set the criteria for success based upon existing data or trial implementation. If that takes place, most faculty groups will be satisfied with what *is*(as reflected in the original data) and not what *ought* to be.

Figure 35

Primary and Secondary Criteria for Success

Primary - Minimum Overall Score, Rating, Response Expected if Program/Unit Functioning at an Acceptable Level

Secondary - More Detailed Minimum Subscale or Item Score Below Which Faculty/Staff Need to Review to Ascertain Cause and Make Improvement

---

Criteria for success are often set at both the *Primary* (overall) and *Secondary* (detailed) levels as reference points or benchmarks for program performance (see Figure 35). The primary criteria for success establish the overall target for general education program performance such as "Average Rating of 85 or Higher" (see Figure 36). The potential use of results for general education program improvement can be *greatly enhanced* by setting secondary criteria for success that require more detailed analysis such as "On no component will average score be less than seven" (also see Figure 36). While overall general education performance may meet or exceed the primary criteria for success, faculty are informed through consideration of the secondary analysis of those more specific areas, scales, or individual items falling short of their expectations. Whenever feasible, faculty should set not only mary, but secondary criteria for success and conduct detailed analysis of assessment information to the level necessary for it to be of use.

Figure 36

Oral Communication Evaluation Sheet

Material Organization	Points
Subject	1-10
Logical Organization	1-10
Content	1-10
Supporting Material	1-10

Delivery and Presentation

Voice and Enunciation	1-10
Language	1-10
Gestures	1-10
Eye Contact	1-10

Overall Effectiveness

Audience Appeal	1-10
Speaker Attitude	1-10
Total	10-100

Criteria for Success

Primary Criteria

Average Rating 85 or Higher

Secondary Criteria

On No Component will Average Score be Less Than Seven

Concluding Comments and Examples of the Means of Assessment for General Education

Figures 37-39 continue the development of the models earlier introduced in Figures 14-16 (pages 34-35) and represent *assessment plans* concerning general education for various types of institutions. In each case, specific means of assessment are directly associated with the individual intended educational outcomes for the general education programs contained in these earlier figures. It should also be noted that on most occasions multiple means of assessment are indicated for each outcome. This action is advised by regional accrediting associations and is based upon the developmental nature of many assessment activities. Appendix "A", describing the means of assessment often associated with differing types of general education outcomes, extends the guidance provided by these models. Also note that both primary and, where appropriate, secondary criteria for success have been identified concerning means of assessment. It must be borne in mind that these assessment plans represent only an intermediate stop on the route to conducting assessment activities and utilizing the data obtained for the improvement of the institution's general education program.

Figure 37

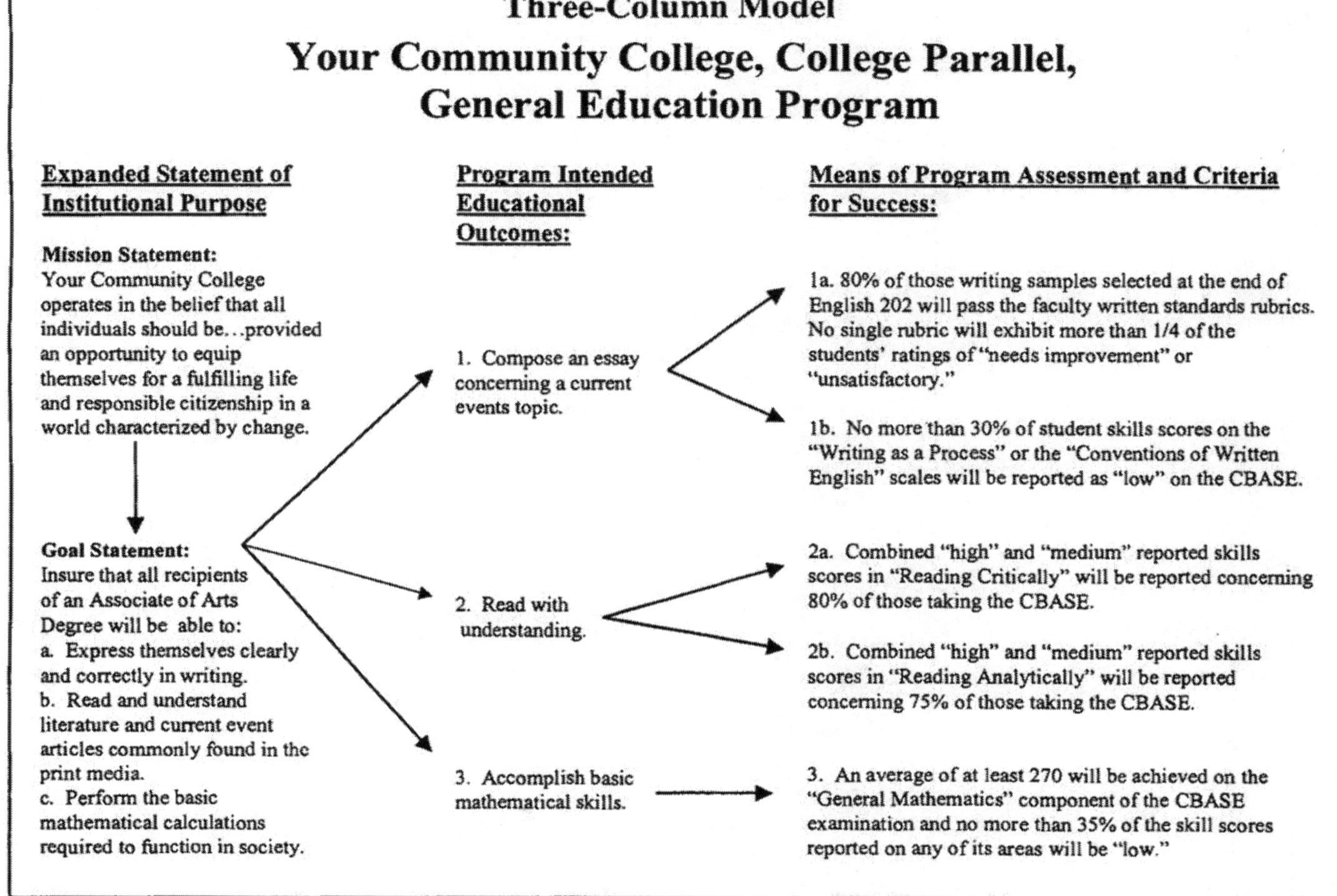

Three-Column Model

Your Community College, College Parallel,
General Education Program

Expanded Statement of Institutional Purpose

Program Intended Educational Outcomes:

Means of Program Assessment and Criteria for Success:

Mission Statement:
Your Community College operates in the belief that all individuals should be…provided an opportunity to equip themselves for a fulfilling life and responsible citizenship in a world characterized by change.

Goal Statement:
Insure that all recipients of an Associate of Arts Degree will be able to:
a. Express themselves clearly and correctly in writing.
b. Read and understand literature and current event articles commonly found in the print media.
c. Perform the basic mathematical calculations required to function in society.

1. Compose an essay concerning a current events topic.

2. Read with understanding.

3. Accomplish basic mathematical skills.

1a. 80% of those writing samples selected at the end of English 202 will pass the faculty written standards rubrics. No single rubric will exhibit more than 1/4 of the students' ratings of "needs improvement" or "unsatisfactory."

1b. No more than 30% of student skills scores on the "Writing as a Process" or the "Conventions of Written English" scales will be reported as "low" on the CBASE.

2a. Combined "high" and "medium" reported skills scores in "Reading Critically" will be reported concerning 80% of those taking the CBASE.

2b. Combined "high" and "medium" reported skills scores in "Reading Analytically" will be reported concerning 75% of those taking the CBASE.

3. An average of at least 270 will be achieved on the "General Mathematics" component of the CBASE examination and no more than 35% of the skill scores reported on any of its areas will be "low."

Figure 38

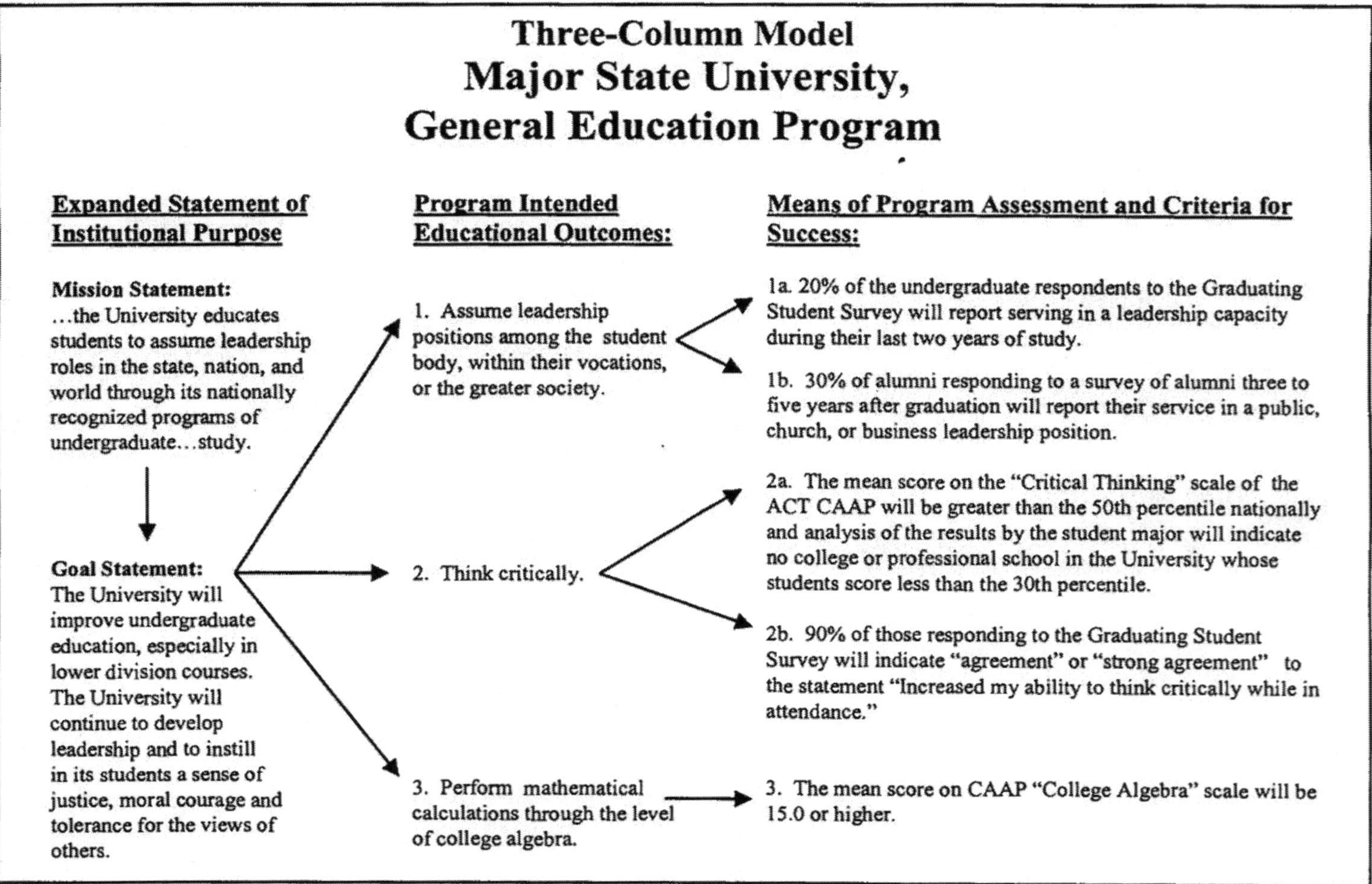

Three-Column Model
Major State University,
General Education Program

Expanded Statement of Institutional Purpose

Program Intended Educational Outcomes:

Means of Program Assessment and Criteria for Success:

Mission Statement:
...the University educates students to assume leadership roles in the state, nation, and world through its nationally recognized programs of undergraduate...study.

Goal Statement:
The University will improve undergraduate education, especially in lower division courses. The University will continue to develop leadership and to instill in its students a sense of justice, moral courage and tolerance for the views of others.

1. Assume leadership positions among the student body, within their vocations, or the greater society.

2. Think critically.

3. Perform mathematical calculations through the level of college algebra.

1a. 20% of the undergraduate respondents to the Graduating Student Survey will report serving in a leadership capacity during their last two years of study.

1b. 30% of alumni responding to a survey of alumni three to five years after graduation will report their service in a public, church, or business leadership position.

2a. The mean score on the "Critical Thinking" scale of the ACT CAAP will be greater than the 50th percentile nationally and analysis of the results by the student major will indicate no college or professional school in the University whose students score less than the 30th percentile.

2b. 90% of those responding to the Graduating Student Survey will indicate "agreement" or "strong agreement" to the statement "Increased my ability to think critically while in attendance."

3. The mean score on CAAP "College Algebra" scale will be 15.0 or higher.

Figure 39

Three-Column Model
Private University,
General Education Program

Expanded Statement of Institutional Purpose

Program Intended Educational Outcomes:

Means of Program Assessment and Criteria for Success:

Mission Statement:
Students can realize the full potential of their abilities and come to understand their responsibility for service in the human community.

Goal Statement:
Graduates will be able to:
a. Express themselves clearly, correctly and succinctly in writing.
b. Make an effective verbal presentation of their ideas concerning a topic.
c. Read and offer an analysis of periodical literature concerning a topic of interest.
d. Complete accurately basic mathematical calculations.
e. Demonstrate a sufficient level of computer literacy.
f. Act in accordance with commonly accepted Judeo-Christian values.

1. Demonstrate their mastery of basic computer skills.

2. Make effective verbal presentations.

3. Act in such a way as to demonstrate their commitment to commonly accepted Judeo-Christian values.

1a. The scores of 85% of students taking the locally developed performance test for the first time at the end of CS 208 (a required course) will be judged as acceptable and on no individual item on the thirty item list prepared by the faculty will the institutional average score be less than 3.5 on a 5.0 scale.
1b. All majors will complete a senior project during their required capstone course. The projects will be sampled and 70% will be judged by computer science faculty to exhibit "a substantial portion" of the skills earlier identified in the institution's thirty item "computer skills checklist."

2a. An average score of 85 will result when student presentations at the close of Speech 175 (a required course) are sampled by video tape and evaluated by a panel of faculty using the Oral Communication Evaluation Sheet and on no component will the average score be less than 7.0 on the 1-10 scale utilized.
2b. 90% of those responding to the Graduating Student Survey will indicate "agreement" or "strong agreement" with the statement "I am confident in my ability to speak in front of an audience."

3a. When faced with a moral dilemma as part of the case study required in each major's capstone course, 80% of the graduating class will choose a solution identified by the faculty as that demonstrating a commitment to Judeo-Christian beliefs.
3b. The average monthly attendance at church reported on the recent alumni survey will exceed 2.5 times per month.

CHAPTER V

CONDUCTING ASSESSMENT IN GENERAL EDUCATION

There should be centralized coordination, guidance and support of assessment in general education. However, the assessment activities themselves may either be centralized or decentralized.

Central guidance and coordination of assessment activities should be provided by the general education assessment committee identified in Chapter II. Otherwise, individual departments will tend to go their own way, with the result that there will probably be gaps in coverage of outcomes, overlaps regarding other outcomes, and duplication of effort.

While centralized guidance and coordination is necessary, execution of many (if not most) assessment activities is decentralized to the department level. In the case of general education, "department level" may easily be dispersed across the number of disciplines described in the catalogue as providing the service courses for the general education curriculum. While some support for this decentralized execution of the general education assessment plan will necessarily be provided by the institution level (standardized testing in general education, the conduct of surveys regarding the subject, etc.), other aspects of general education assessment are uniquely accomplished within each discipline. These might include the videotaping of oral communication presentations, collection of writing samples, etc.

There are a number of logistical considerations concerning assessment in general education which the institution needs to address. These are shown in Figure 40. Among the initial decisions which will need to be reached in conducting general education assessment is one concerning whether the entire population of students eligible or a sample thereof should be utilized for assessment of general education. It is necessary to understand that only a *representative sample* of general education program completers is required since the focus of our assessment program is on general education rather than on individual students. Such sampling is an attractive alternative (particularly when considering the cost implications) and, as long as the sample can be defended as representative (not necessarily random) of program completers as a whole, there should be no challenge to the procedure. Institutions will need to be able to defend the sample chosen based upon the students' entering admissions or diagnostic scores, high school grade point averages, and institutional

GPAs (as well as representativeness of the sample by race, gender, full-time, part-time enrollment status, etc.) compared to the population. However, at an institution with a relatively small number (100 or less) of students completing the general education program each year, the population is probably the best choice in this matter.

Figure 40

Logistical Considerations in General Education Assessment

- Sample or Population

- Identification of Transfer Students

- Selection of Students to be Assessed

- Time for Assessment Activities

- Student Motivation

- Distribution of Results

How large a sample should be taken of those students completing the general education program? Given probable institutional fiscal and logistical constraints, a representative sample as small as 30% of the population will probably be sufficient for the purpose of making overall judgments concerning the effectiveness of the general education program. From a statistical standpoint, users of these data will have to be aware of limitations (such as potential sample bias) resulting from such a limited number of responses. However, the ability to draw truly random samples from a highly independent undergraduate group of students is next to impossible without heavy-handed means that are rejected by most campuses. Additionally, many institutions do not consider favorably a suggestion that all students be required to go through assessment activities such as a three-hour standardized test in general education.

The identification of students in the sample or population *receiving the bulk of their general education from the institution* is essential. Colleges generally desire not to take the blame for those students transferring into the institution large amounts of their general education programming from another institution such as a community college (neither should the institution take credit for that education). For that reason, institutions will need either to (a) exclude students from the group assessed that have a given number of hours or more of their general education courses taken at other institutions or (b) include transfer students in the population or sample, but be able to sort the results based upon locally defined "native students" and those who have transferred significant amounts of their programming from other institutions. In the authors' opinion, this latter approach is preferable. It is not unheard of for transfer students to score better in the assessment process than an institution's native students. Needless to say, this raises a host of questions at the institution conducting the assessment.

Just exactly whom do we include in our general education assessment effort? Most institutions choose to conduct assessment of general education for "rising juniors." These students have completed most of two years of undergraduate instruction at the institution and often are identified as having obtained between 45 and 70 semester credit hours.

Another approach to assessment in general education available to four-year institutions is to wait until the end of the students' baccalaureate programming to conduct assessment of general education. The assumption supporting this course of action is that by that time students will have taken all general education courses. Institutions choosing this alternative need to make sure that any normative-based assessment comparison is referenced to other institutions also conducting assessment of general education at the end of the baccalaureate program. Otherwise, an inappropriate (but probably very satisfying) comparison will result.

Creation of a specific time during which to accomplish the assessment of general education offers a number of alternatives. Many institutions choose either the end of the spring semester or the beginning of the fall semester to create an "assessment day" during which time various assessment activities, including those in general education, can take place. Often students are encouraged to participate in these activities by not allowing them to register for classes without having taken part.

Another choice concerning the time designated for general education assessment relates to its accomplishment *within* or *outside* scheduled class periods. Some of the means of general education assessment, most notably standardized testing, require between two and four hours of students' time and are therefore very difficult to integrate into the standard class schedule. The creation of a separate time such as "on Saturday morning" is a partial solution to this problem because students in large numbers loathe giving up a portion of their weekend for this purpose. It is probably preferable to conduct assessment activities to the maximum extent possible within standard class periods. This may be accomplished, in many cases, by administration of modules or portions of longer means of assessment (such as standardized tests) separately within different classes. This approach has the added benefit of motivating students to complete or take the means of assessment more seriously if they believe their grade in the class is at least to some extent influenced by the assessment process. Frequently, course-embedded means of assessment such as oral presentations and writing samples may be taken from individual classes without additional requirements or time being asked of the students.

Figure 41

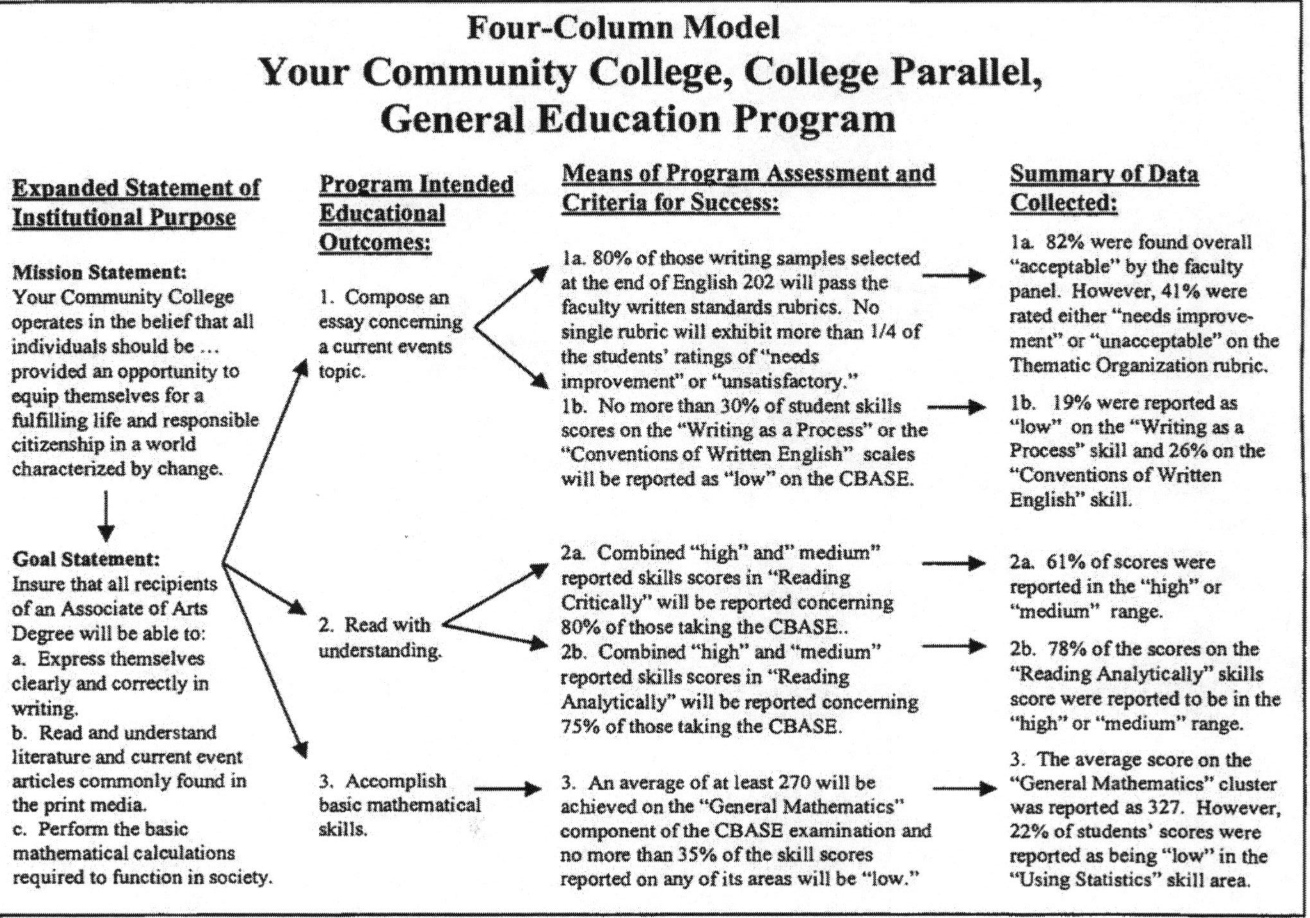

Four-Column Model
Your Community College, College Parallel,
General Education Program

Expanded Statement of Institutional Purpose

Mission Statement:
Your Community College operates in the belief that all individuals should be … provided an opportunity to equip themselves for a fulfilling life and responsible citizenship in a world characterized by change.

Goal Statement:
Insure that all recipients of an Associate of Arts Degree will be able to:
a. Express themselves clearly and correctly in writing.
b. Read and understand literature and current event articles commonly found in the print media.
c. Perform the basic mathematical calculations required to function in society.

Program Intended Educational Outcomes:

1. Compose an essay concerning a current events topic.

2. Read with understanding.

3. Accomplish basic mathematical skills.

Means of Program Assessment and Criteria for Success:

1a. 80% of those writing samples selected at the end of English 202 will pass the faculty written standards rubrics. No single rubric will exhibit more than 1/4 of the students' ratings of "needs improvement" or "unsatisfactory."
1b. No more than 30% of student skills scores on the "Writing as a Process" or the "Conventions of Written English" scales will be reported as "low" on the CBASE.

2a. Combined "high" and "medium" reported skills scores in "Reading Critically" will be reported concerning 80% of those taking the CBASE..
2b. Combined "high" and "medium" reported skills scores in "Reading Analytically" will be reported concerning 75% of those taking the CBASE.

3. An average of at least 270 will be achieved on the "General Mathematics" component of the CBASE examination and no more than 35% of the skill scores reported on any of its areas will be "low."

Summary of Data Collected:

1a. 82% were found overall "acceptable" by the faculty panel. However, 41% were rated either "needs improvement" or "unacceptable" on the Thematic Organization rubric.
1b. 19% were reported as "low" on the "Writing as a Process" skill and 26% on the "Conventions of Written English" skill.

2a. 61% of scores were reported in the "high" or "medium" range.
2b. 78% of the scores on the "Reading Analytically" skills score were reported to be in the "high" or "medium" range.

3. The average score on the "General Mathematics" cluster was reported as 327. However, 22% of students' scores were reported as being "low" in the "Using Statistics" skill area.

Figure 42

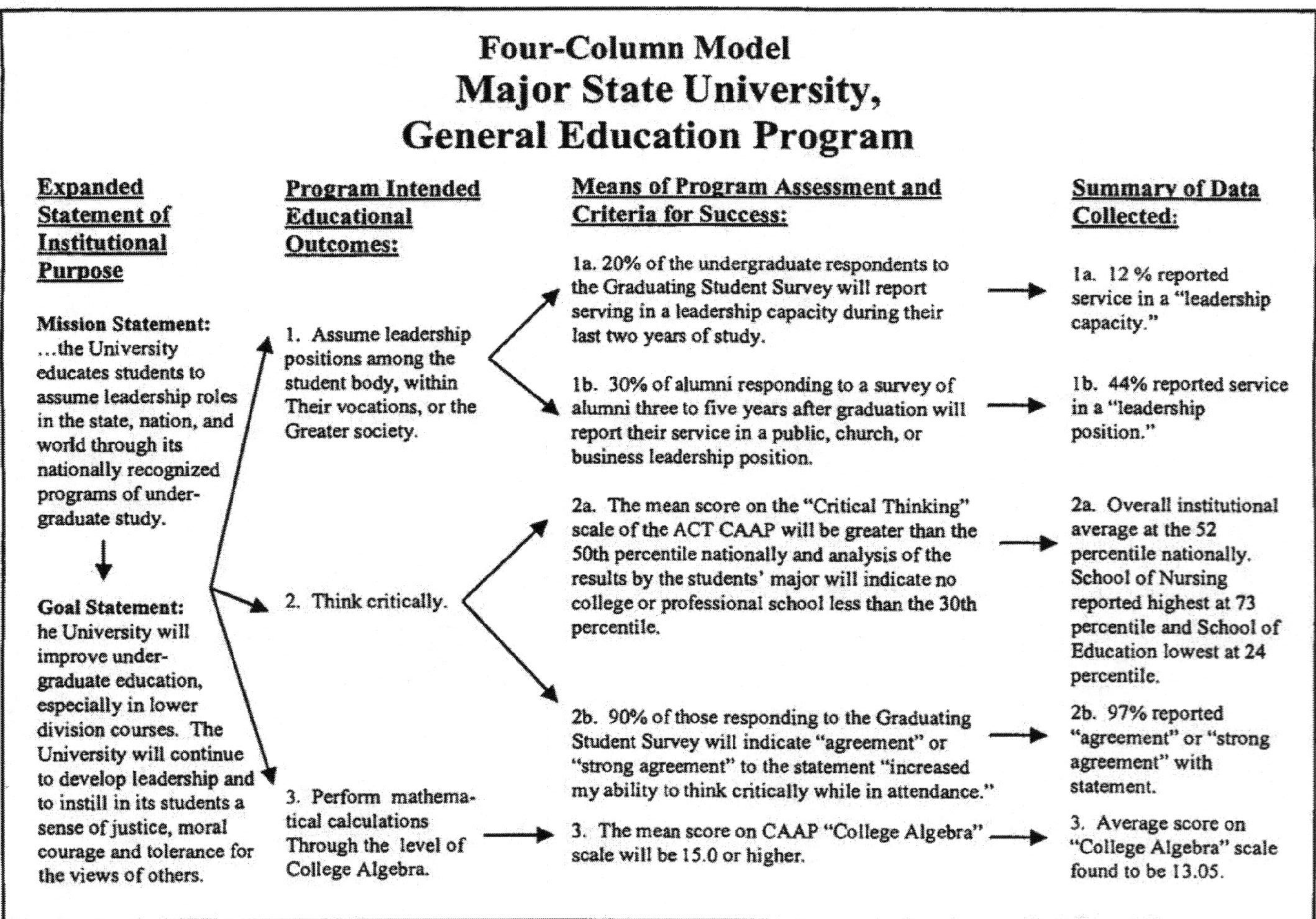

Four-Column Model
Major State University,
General Education Program

Expanded Statement of Institutional Purpose

Program Intended Educational Outcomes:

Means of Program Assessment and Criteria for Success:

Summary of Data Collected:

Mission Statement: …the University educates students to assume leadership roles in the state, nation, and world through its nationally recognized programs of under-graduate study.

Goal Statement: he University will improve under-graduate education, especially in lower division courses. The University will continue to develop leadership and to instill in its students a sense of justice, moral courage and tolerance for the views of others.

1. Assume leadership positions among the student body, within Their vocations, or the Greater society.

2. Think critically.

3. Perform mathema-tical calculations Through the level of College Algebra.

1a. 20% of the undergraduate respondents to the Graduating Student Survey will report serving in a leadership capacity during their last two years of study.

1b. 30% of alumni responding to a survey of alumni three to five years after graduation will report their service in a public, church, or business leadership position.

2a. The mean score on the "Critical Thinking" scale of the ACT CAAP will be greater than the 50th percentile nationally and analysis of the results by the students' major will indicate no college or professional school less than the 30th percentile.

2b. 90% of those responding to the Graduating Student Survey will indicate "agreement" or "strong agreement" to the statement "increased my ability to think critically while in attendance."

3. The mean score on CAAP "College Algebra" scale will be 15.0 or higher.

1a. 12 % reported service in a "leadership capacity."

1b. 44% reported service in a "leadership position."

2a. Overall institutional average at the 52 percentile nationally. School of Nursing reported highest at 73 percentile and School of Education lowest at 24 percentile.

2b. 97% reported "agreement" or "strong agreement" with statement.

3. Average score on "College Algebra" scale found to be 13.05.

Figure 43

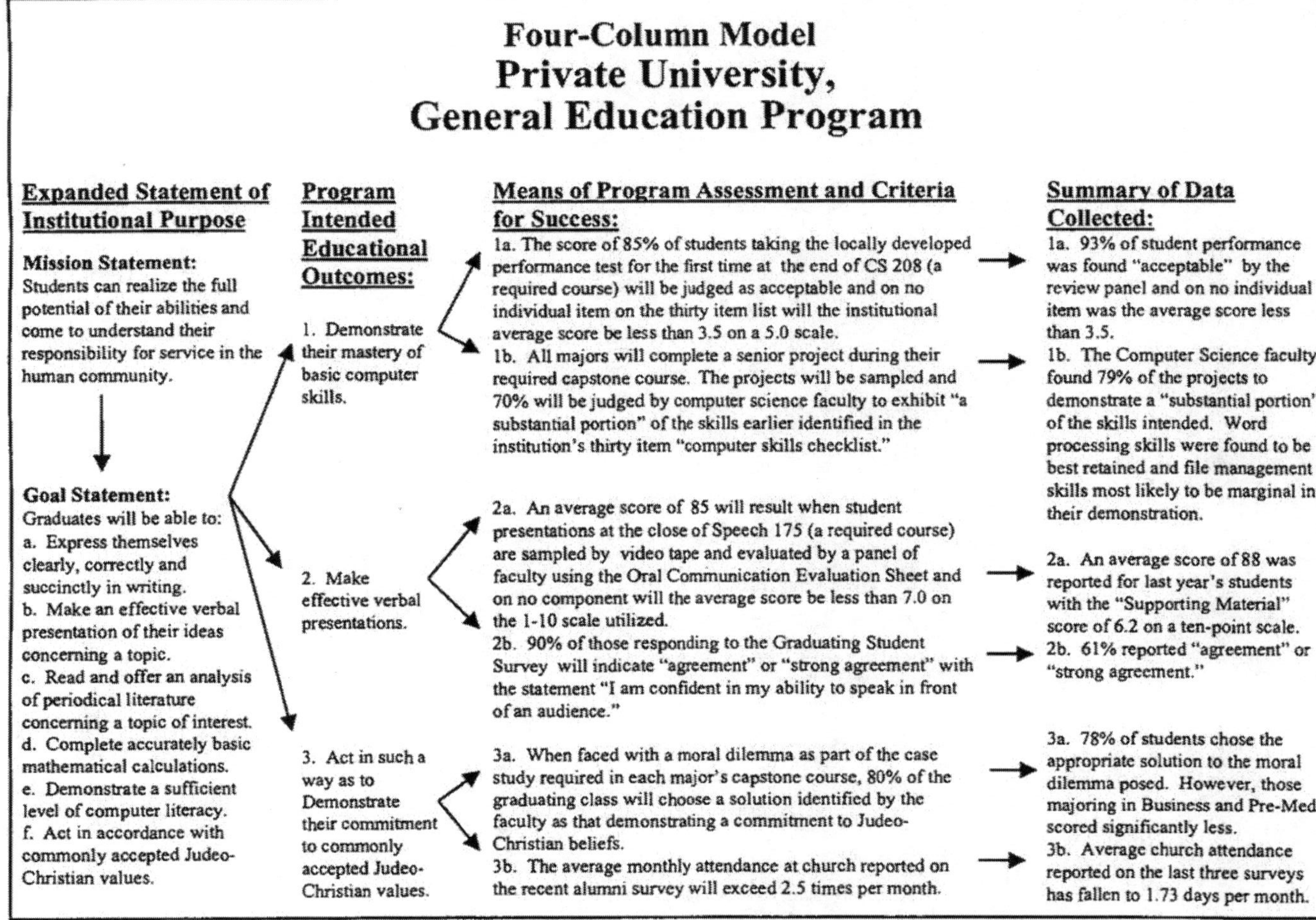

Four-Column Model
Private University,
General Education Program

Expanded Statement of Institutional Purpose

Mission Statement:
Students can realize the full potential of their abilities and come to understand their responsibility for service in the human community.

Goal Statement:
Graduates will be able to:
a. Express themselves clearly, correctly and succinctly in writing.
b. Make an effective verbal presentation of their ideas concerning a topic.
c. Read and offer an analysis of periodical literature concerning a topic of interest.
d. Complete accurately basic mathematical calculations.
e. Demonstrate a sufficient level of computer literacy.
f. Act in accordance with commonly accepted Judeo-Christian values.

Program Intended Educational Outcomes:

1. Demonstrate their mastery of basic computer skills.

2. Make effective verbal presentations.

3. Act in such a way as to Demonstrate their commitment to commonly accepted Judeo-Christian values.

Means of Program Assessment and Criteria for Success:

1a. The score of 85% of students taking the locally developed performance test for the first time at the end of CS 208 (a required course) will be judged as acceptable and on no individual item on the thirty item list will the institutional average score be less than 3.5 on a 5.0 scale.
1b. All majors will complete a senior project during their required capstone course. The projects will be sampled and 70% will be judged by computer science faculty to exhibit "a substantial portion" of the skills earlier identified in the institution's thirty item "computer skills checklist."

2a. An average score of 85 will result when student presentations at the close of Speech 175 (a required course) are sampled by video tape and evaluated by a panel of faculty using the Oral Communication Evaluation Sheet and on no component will the average score be less than 7.0 on the 1-10 scale utilized.
2b. 90% of those responding to the Graduating Student Survey will indicate "agreement" or "strong agreement" with the statement "I am confident in my ability to speak in front of an audience."

3a. When faced with a moral dilemma as part of the case study required in each major's capstone course, 80% of the graduating class will choose a solution identified by the faculty as that demonstrating a commitment to Judeo-Christian beliefs.
3b. The average monthly attendance at church reported on the recent alumni survey will exceed 2.5 times per month.

Summary of Data Collected:

1a. 93% of student performance was found "acceptable" by the review panel and on no individual item was the average score less than 3.5.
1b. The Computer Science faculty found 79% of the projects to demonstrate a "substantial portion" of the skills intended. Word processing skills were found to be best retained and file management skills most likely to be marginal in their demonstration.

2a. An average score of 88 was reported for last year's students with the "Supporting Material" score of 6.2 on a ten-point scale.
2b. 61% reported "agreement" or "strong agreement."

3a. 78% of students chose the appropriate solution to the moral dilemma posed. However, those majoring in Business and Pre-Med. scored significantly less.
3b. Average church attendance reported on the last three surveys has fallen to 1.73 days per month.

Students can be required to participate in assessment of general education, or for that matter any other form of assessment, in fulfillment of catalog requirements. Unfortunately students cannot be required to take assessment activities *seriously*. See pages 45-46 for suggestions regarding improvement of student motivation to actively and seriously take part in assessment activities.

General education assessment results should be distributed to both the centralized committee overseeing the process as well as the individual departments concerned with each outcome. While little corrective action should be expected from the coordinating committee, the departments directly associated with the outcomes, means of assessment, etc., should be expected to use the results for the improvement of student learning.

Shown in Figures 41-43 (pages 71-73) are the four-column models, which highlight the results of assessment activities (under the column head "Summary of Data"), earlier identified in Figures 37-39 (pages 65-67). These assessment results should logically flow from the means of assessment identified and measure or assess the accomplishments of the outcomes to which they are linked. (In actual practice, more information regarding the results of the measurement process are frequently reported using the Assessment Record Book forms described in Chapter VII).

Figure 44

Assessment Results Presented *Should*:

- ### Highlight the Extent to Which Outcomes Were Accomplished

- ### Appear to Have Resulted from the Means of Assessment Earlier Described

- ### Be in Sufficient Detail to Convince the Reader That Assessment Actually Took Place

- ### Justify the "Use of Results" Later Identified

The summary of assessment data reported should meet the criteria shown in Figure 44. Assessment results presented should focus upon and highlight the extent to which the outcome was accomplished. Data concerning the extent to which the primary criterion for success was achieved should be provided. In addition, a brief review and identification of any areas in which the secondary criteria for success were not met should also be provided.

While it may appear to be unnecessary to say, the assessment results provided should appear to have logically resulted from the means of assessment earlier described. In numerous cases, the authors have reviewed assessment reports in which the summary of data provided actually resulted from other than the means of assessment described in the third column.

There should be enough detail provided concerning the results of the assessment process to convince the reader that assessment actually took place. Very brief or vague reports of findings such as "criteria for success met" are sure to encourage the reader to ask for a review of all the detailed data and at the same time reflect poorly upon the institution's credibility. The summary of assessment data presented should provide specific results such as actual averages, percentages, etc.

Finally, the assessment results provided should logically justify the use of results later described. The assessment results included in column four can be viewed as "laying the foundation" for the change made later under the title "use of results."

Figure 45

Assessment Results Presented *Should Not:*

- Exactly Match Criteria for Success Cited

- Be Reported in Round Numbers Unless Very Small Numbers Are Involved

- Be Statistically Impossible or Unlikely

There are clearly a number of characteristics which the assessment results should not display (see Figure 45). Assessment results that *exactly match* the criteria for success reflected in the third column cause the reader to question the credibility of the data cited. Practitioners understand that assessment research very seldom results in "round numbers" unless very small numbers of observations are involved. Assessment data reported as 50%, 75%, 80%, 100% should be explained by also citing the number of observations (4 of 5, 3 of 4, etc.) to increase confidence on the part of the reader. Finally, the assessment results presented should be statistically possible. The authors are reminded of one report they were asked to review in which

"80% of the seven program completers" were reported as achieving a certain identical score on a standardized test. First, statistically 80% of seven participants would be 5.6 participants. Second, it is highly unlikely that 80% of any number of examination scores would be *exactly* the same.

It is extremely likely that general education assessment activities will take several years to fully implement. The authors suggest implementation of procedures first on a pilot basis with a portion of general education program completers whenever possible. Such pilot implementation will identify logistical, student motivation, and instrumentation problems on a small scale before full implementation on a much greater scale. Nonetheless, institutions should implement the measures identified as expeditiously as possible so as to move toward the use of assessment results described in the next chapter.

CHAPTER VI

USING ASSESSMENT INFORMATION TO IMPROVE GENERAL EDUCATION PROGRAMMING

Both the committee coordinating general education assessment and the individual academic departments whose course offerings support the program play a role in the use of assessment information to improve general education. The role of the committee coordinating general education assessment is exactly that, *coordination*. The committee can see that the data are utilized, monitor use of data regarding cross disciplinary outcomes such as critical thinking, and ensure that uses of the data in one discipline do not have an adverse impact upon others. However, the bulk of the substantive use of general education assessment information takes place within the academic departments providing the courses, which compose the general education program. It is within these academic departments that course syllabi are adjusted, means of instruction changed, and other actions are taken which directly affect the student and result in an improved general education program and student learning. Within these departments any number of obstacles to use of these results can be encountered.

Figure 46 outlines a number of roadblocks to the use of assessment results in general education. While most faculty are not wildly enthusiastic about assessment and the use of results for improvement in their majors, there is often apparently even more reluctance regarding change in general education. This reluctance is due to many of the roadblocks next discussed.

Because of the need for a central coordinating body or committee regarding the overall general education program, there is less singular and direct responsibility for use of results lodged with individual academic departments. In most institutional general education assessment models, an individual academic department has no more than one outcome (writing, math, etc.) in which it has the primary interest or responsibility. This is unlike assessment in the major, where total responsibility is usually fixed upon an individual academic department. In general education, a single department "owns" only a portion of the general education outcomes program. This dispersion of responsibility often leads to less attention by each discipline than would otherwise occur.

Figure 46

Roadblocks to Use of Assessment Results in General Education

1. Complexity of Responsibility Structure

2. Multidisciplinary Outcomes

3. Nature of Disciplines Involved

4. Lack of Confidence in Means of Assessment

Multidisciplinary outcomes further complicate issues regarding responsibility and the use of data. Outcomes such as critical thinking, logical reasoning, and commitment to ethnic and gender diversity require action on a broad front involving many departments. It is not necessary that every department use assessment results to improve critical thinking every year. However, the institution will need to go about sequencing or scheduling different departments to focus upon multidisciplinary outcomes in their results periodically. This type of coordination and sequencing can best be orchestrated by the general education assessment committee.

The disciplines involved in support or service of general education requirements, (particularly those in the humanities, social sciences, fine and performing arts) are not among those whose orientation leads naturally to the scientific method in which change is based upon data (see earlier comments in Chapter I). Further, many of these disciplines lack experience with assessment requirements of professional accrediting associations. These disciplines may also generally be described as "lacking confidence in quantitative means of assessment," as a basis for changing of their disciplines. This lack of confidence is reinforced by both disciplinary cynicism regarding any standardized test as dictating program content and the nature of some (if not most) standardized tests of general education.

Given the roadblocks cited above, how can an institution go about facilitating use of assessment results concerning general education programs? While there are no instant solutions to the roadblocks there are a number of actions that can help to limit their impact.

While the responsibility structure including both the institutional general education assessment committee and the individual disciplines or departments may be somewhat complex, it will substantially facilitate use of results if the various responsibilities of each group are clearly articulated. The general education assessment committee should be charged with establishing a timeline by which assessment should be accomplished and data utilized for program improvement purposes and then monitoring to see that those actions actually take place. The disciplines involved should be clearly charged with analyzing the assessment results in their fields and implementing the necessary steps to improve student learning.

The nature of many general education outcomes is multidisciplinary in nature and there should be no attempt to change or simplify what are indeed complex concepts such as "critical thinking." It will facilitate utilization of results if individual disciplines can identify portions of their courses that support multidisciplinary outcomes such as critical thinking. Thereby, when assessment results are received students passing through the various classes can be tracked to determine their ability in each of the multidisciplinary outcomes cited. If one approach in a particular discipline is supportive of students gaining the ability to "think critically" then faculty may wish to emulate that approach in their own discipline.

Building the confidence of faculty in the means of assessment utilized for general education is essential if the results are to be utilized to improve programs. This can best be accomplished by delegating to the faculty in the disciplines the responsibility for identifying the means of assessment for those outcomes related to their discipline. In most cases, this will initially result in the rejection of standardized approaches and the development of locally developed means of assessment in which the faculty (because they were involved in the design) have a greater degree of confidence. This approach is entirely acceptable; however, the authors suggest that the individual discipline research designs and research results be made known to the campus general education assessment committee. Standardized means of assessment may appear more acceptable once the magnitude of effort in local development is encountered.

Assessment results are normally utilized in general education (as well as assessment in the major) to make changes in what we teach and how it is taught. In the field of general education, the adjustments regarding "what we teach" will certainly be evolutionary rather than revolutionary in nature. In most cases, changes concerning a discipline will be accomplished by the updating of material, refocusing of content within courses, or the broadening of distribution requirements within the discipline to enable students to take other courses to satisfy the general education requirement.

Changes in "how we teach" in general education are among the most common changes and primarily result in more active involvement of students in learning through application of the various subjects, rather than rote memorization of facts. Additionally, students may be required to utilize automated means (word processing, spreadsheets, etc.) as part of their courses in order to demonstrate their competency in computer applications.

Figures 47-49 depict completed five-column models for each of the general education programs at different types of institutions discussed in this publication. The use of results described in actual documentation on your campus will be somewhat more detailed than those shown in these models as the authors suggest utilization of the Assessment Record Book procedure described in the following chapter to document the overall process. The Assessment Record Book forms provide substantially more room to describe the use of results than the five column models presented.

Figure 47

Five-Column Model
Your Community College, College Parallel, General Education Program

Expanded Statement of Institutional Purpose	Program Intended Educational Outcomes:	Means of Program Assessment and Criteria for Success:	Summary of Data Collected:	Use of Results:
Mission Statement: Your Community College operates in the belief that all individuals should be…provided an opportunity to equip themselves for a fulfilling life and responsible citizenship in a world characterized by change.	1. Compose an essay concerning a current events topic.	1a. 80% of those writing samples selected at the end of English 202 will pass the faculty written standards rubrics. No single rubric will exhibit more than 1/4 of the students' ratings of "needs improvement" or "unsatisfactory." 1b. No more than 30% of student skills scores on the "Writing as a Process" or the "Conventions of Written English" scales will be reported as "low" on the CBASE..	1a. 82% were found overall "acceptable" by the faculty panel. However, 41% were rated either "needs improvement" or "unacceptable" on the Thematic Organization rubric. 1b. 19% were reported as "low" on the "writing as a process" skill and 26% on the "Conventions of Written English" skill.	1a. "Thematic Organization" rubric now emphasized in critique of English Comp I and II classes. 1b. Match of the "Conventions of Written English" skill area on CBASE with course syllabi reviewed. Additional collaboration with "Writing Center" has doubled the number of student writing examples reviewed in Comp I & II.
Goal Statement: Insure that all recipients of an Associate of Arts Degree will be able to: a. Express themselves clearly and correctly in writing. b. Read and under-stand literature and current event articles commonly found in the print media. c. Perform the basic mathematical calculations required to function in society.	2. Read with understanding.	2a. Combined "high" and "medium" reported skills scores in "Reading Critically" will be reported concerning 80% of those taking the CBASE. 2b. Combined "high" and "medium" reported skills scores in "Reading Analytically" will be reported concerning 75% of those taking the CBASE.	2a. 61% of scores were reported in the "high" or "medium" range. 2b. 78% of the scores on the "Reading Analytically" skills score were reported to be in the "high" or "medium" range.	2a. History 106, Literature 105, Political Science 202, modified to require students on several occasions to read a passage critically, recognizing assumptions and implications, and evaluating ideas. 2b. No action this academic year, continue to monitor.
	3. Accomplish basic mathematical skills.	3. An average of at least 270 will be achieved on the "General Mathematics" component of the CBASE examination and no more than 35% of the skill scores reported on any of its areas will be "low."	3. The average score on the "General Mathematics" cluster was reported as 327. However, 27% of students' scores were reported as being "low" in the "Using Statistics" skill area.	3. Math 107, Quantitative Reasoning, is now required for all college parallel students.

Figure 48

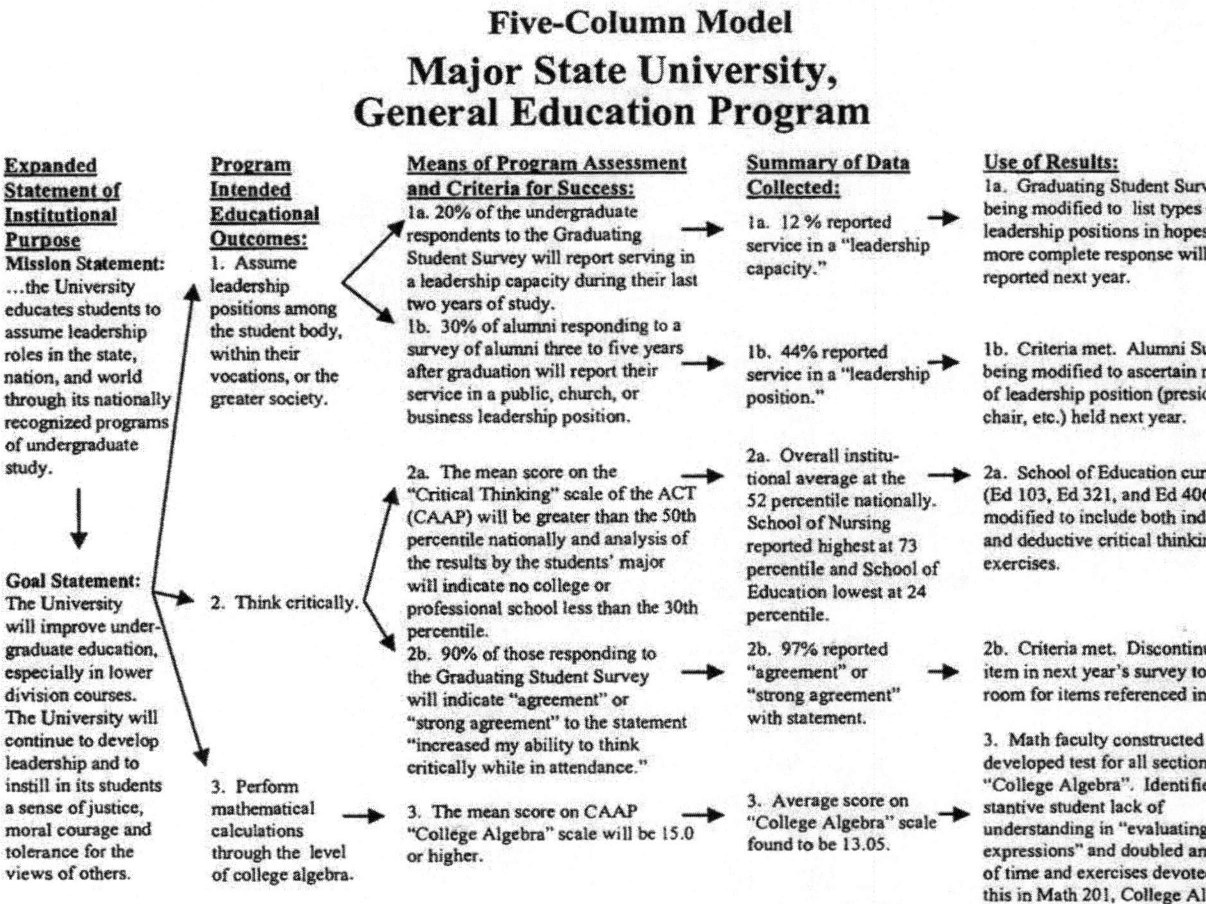

Five-Column Model
Major State University,
General Education Program

Expanded Statement of Institutional Purpose
Mission Statement: …the University educates students to assume leadership roles in the state, nation, and world through its nationally recognized programs of undergraduate study.

Goal Statement: The University will improve under-graduate education, especially in lower division courses. The University will continue to develop leadership and to instill in its students a sense of justice, moral courage and tolerance for the views of others.

Program Intended Educational Outcomes:
1. Assume leadership positions among the student body, within their vocations, or the greater society.

2. Think critically.

3. Perform mathematical calculations through the level of college algebra.

Means of Program Assessment and Criteria for Success:
1a. 20% of the undergraduate respondents to the Graduating Student Survey will report serving in a leadership capacity during their last two years of study.
1b. 30% of alumni responding to a survey of alumni three to five years after graduation will report their service in a public, church, or business leadership position.

2a. The mean score on the "Critical Thinking" scale of the ACT (CAAP) will be greater than the 50th percentile nationally and analysis of the results by the students' major will indicate no college or professional school less than the 30th percentile.
2b. 90% of those responding to the Graduating Student Survey will indicate "agreement" or "strong agreement" to the statement "increased my ability to think critically while in attendance."

3. The mean score on CAAP "College Algebra" scale will be 15.0 or higher.

Summary of Data Collected:
1a. 12 % reported service in a "leadership capacity."

1b. 44% reported service in a "leadership position."

2a. Overall institu-tional average at the 52 percentile nationally. School of Nursing reported highest at 73 percentile and School of Education lowest at 24 percentile.

2b. 97% reported "agreement" or "strong agreement" with statement.

3. Average score on "College Algebra" scale found to be 13.05.

Use of Results:
1a. Graduating Student Survey being modified to list types of leadership positions in hopes that more complete response will be reported next year.

1b. Criteria met. Alumni Survey being modified to ascertain nature of leadership position (president, chair, etc.) held next year.

2a. School of Education curriculum (Ed 103, Ed 321, and Ed 406) modified to include both inductive and deductive critical thinking exercises.

2b. Criteria met. Discontinuing item in next year's survey to make room for items referenced in 1a.

3. Math faculty constructed locally developed test for all sections of "College Algebra". Identified sub-stantive student lack of understanding in "evaluating expressions" and doubled amount of time and exercises devoted to this in Math 201, College Algebra.

Figure 49

Five-Column Model
Private University,
General Education Program

Expanded Statement of Institutional Purpose	Program Intended Educational Outcomes:	Means of Program Assessment and Criteria for Success:	Summary of Data Collected:	Use of Results:
Mission Statement: Students can realize the full potential of their abilities and come to understand their responsibility for service in the human community.	1. Demonstrate their mastery of basic computer skills.	1a. The performance of 85% of students taking the locally developed standardized performance test for the first time at the end of CS 208 (a required course) will be judged as acceptable and on no individual item on the thirty item list will the institutional average score be less than 3.5 on a 5.0 scale. 1b. All majors will be required to complete a senior project during their required capstone course. The projects will be sampled and 70% will be judged by computer science faculty to exhibit "a substantial portion" of the skills earlier identified in the institution's thirty item "computer skills checklist."	1a. 93% of student performance was found "acceptable" by the review panel and on no individual item was the average score less than 3.5. 1b. The Computer Science faculty found 79% of the projects to demonstrate a "substantial portion" of the skills intended. Word processing skills were found to be best retained and file management skills most likely to be marginal in their demonstration.	1a. No action required at this time, will continue to monitor. 1b. CS 208 modified to add file management exercise in student's anticipated major.
Goal Statement: Graduates will be able to: a. Express themselves clearly, correctly and succinctly in writing. b. Make an effective verbal presentation of their ideas concerning a topic. c. Read and offer an analysis of periodical literature concerning a topic of interest. d. Complete accurately basic mathematical calculations. e. Demonstrate a sufficient level of computer literacy. f. Act in accordance with commonly accepted Judeo-Christian values.	2. Make effective verbal presentations.	2a. An average score of 85 will result when student presentations at the close of Speech 175 (a required course) are sampled by video tape and evaluated by a panel of faculty using the Oral Communication Evaluation Sheet and on no component will the average score be less than 7.0 on the 1-10 scale utilized. 2b. 90% of those responding to the Graduating Student Survey will indicate "agreement" or "strong agreement" with the statement "I am confident in my ability to speak in front of an audience."	2a. An average score of 88 was reported for last year's students with the "Supporting Material" score of 6.2 on a ten-point scale. 2b. 61% reported "agreement" or "strong agreement."	2a. Importance of "Supporting Material" now pointed out in examples of exemplary presentation shown in Introductory Speech 175 class meetings. Critiques of student presentations during class now emphasizes importance of "Supporting Materials". 2b. Graduating student survey item modified to read "I am able to make effective verbal presentations."
	3. Act in such a way as to demonstrate their commitment to commonly accepted Judeo-Christian values.	3a. When faced with a moral dilemma as part of the case study required in each major's capstone course, 80% of the graduating class will choose the solution identified by the faculty as that demonstrating a commitment to Judeo-Christian beliefs. 3b. The average monthly attendance at religious service reported on the recent alumni survey will exceed 2.5 times per month.	3a. 78% of students chose the appropriate solution to the moral dilemma posed. However, those majoring in Business and Pre-Med. scored significantly less. 3b. Average religious service attendance reported on the last three surveys has fallen to 1.73 days per month.	3a. Business and Pre-Med. have revised curricula to better integrate material linking their field with the institutional commitment to Judeo-Christian beliefs. 3b. Student Life is integrating more denominationally related activities into dormitory programming and social functions.

Use of assessment results reported in column five or on the Assessment Record Book forms explained in the following chapter should exhibit the characteristics shown in Figure 50 and should not exhibit those shown in Figure 51.

Figure 50

Use of Assessment Results Described
Should Be:

- Substantive in Nature
- Stated in the Past Tense

- Responsive to Shortcomings Described in the Assessment Results Reported

- Detailed Enough (Course Number and Nature of Change) to Convince the Reader that the Change Actually Took Place

- Where Necessary, Supported by Evidence of Committee Action or Syllabus Change

Figure 51

Use of Assessment Results Described
Should Not Be:

- A Promise to Consider Making a Change Through Referral to a Committee

- Expected on "Every Occasion" or "Never Needed"

- Stated in the Future Tense

The use of assessment results (frequently described as closing the loop) indicated should be clearly responsive to shortcomings described in the assessment results reported under "Summary of Data." On a number of occasions, the authors have observed institutions reporting as use of assessment results, changes which were indeed beneficial to the program, but which were made based upon the "judgment of the faculty" rather than any systematic assessment of student learning. Regional accrediting associations visiting teams have also been known to severely question uses of results that did not appear to be based upon or responsive to the assessment results cited by the institution.

The uses of assessment results cited should be *substantive* in nature. At this point in the development of the institutional effectiveness process across the country, it is no longer sufficient to "change the cover on the same textbook" or state "no change necessary" repeatedly as the result of assessment. Instead, institutions should be able to demonstrate and report actual changes in curriculum or instructional practices which logically should lead to improved learning or "closing the loop" as shown in the examples provided in Figure 47-49.

The report of utilization of assessment results should be detailed enough to convince a reader that the change actually took place. In most cases, this will require a description on the part of the institution of the nature of the changes and in which courses these changes took place. General descriptions such as "change in syllabus" will not, in most cases, be sufficient to satisfy visiting teams. Often the type of description needed to convince the reader that the change actually took place is only feasible using the Assessment Record Book forms provided in Chapter VII.

On the other hand, it is not necessary to maintain the raw data (surveys, tests, papers, etc.) supporting each change in curriculum or course syllabi resulting from assessment implementation *for the full period of reaffirmation*. Institutions are advised to retain complete documentation (including syllabus changes and committee minutes) in the year just before visitation or in those circumstances in which the institution is submitting a report in response to an adverse finding. This detailed documentation provides credibility to the summary of assessment data contained on the Assessment Record Book forms completed for earlier periods.

Finally, and most importantly, use of assessment results should be stated in the past tense. Regional accreditation representatives have been often promised that assessment results would be utilized in the future only to find that these promises have gone unfulfilled at the next visit. Wherever possible, the use of assessment results should be reported in the past tense. In those cases where changes based upon assessment results are in process, institutions should describe the nature of the process, its status as of the report and the date which the change is anticipated being placed in effect.

Many of the characteristics which use of assessment results *should not* resemble are constituted by the reverse of the characteristics cited in Figure 51. As an example, referral of assessment results to a committee for their consideration can hardly be described as substantive or detailed enough to suffice. However, this approach is not uncommon in reviewing reports of the use of assessment results by the authors. It constitutes a convenient way out of dealing with controversial matters that need to be changed.

The use of assessment results to improve learning should not be necessary on every occasion. However, when institutions report assessment results demonstrating conclusively their achievement of the intended general education outcomes being assessed, they should move the outcome being assessed back to the "long list" and move forward other outcomes for assessment during the next period. While this does not constitute "substantive use of results," it does indicate the sincerity of the process and its systematic and ongoing nature.

Conversely, no general education program, or for that matter major, should report in every instance meeting the criteria for success regarding each outcome established and therefore, not in need of change. Such findings regarding *all* of the outcomes in any one year raise genuine questions regarding the seriousness with which the institution is utilizing the process to bring about program improvement. It is suggested that in each educational program, including *general education,* at least one substantive change in curriculum or teaching methodology be reported every year in order to give the institution's implementation of institutional effectiveness credibility. Setting of secondary criteria for success for several means of assessment should facilitate accomplishment of this suggestion.

Finally, the use of results should not be stated in terms of the future tense. If the institution has established plans for making a change (as opposed to having made the change) a specific sequence of events should be described leading inexorably to program improvement. Funding for the change should be identified and a description of the events already accomplished toward this end should be documented.

The use of assessment results to improve general education programming at the institution is the end result of the entire process described to this point. However, unlike the movie *Field of Dreams,* in which voices from the corn field are heard to say, "If you build it, they will come," having assessment data regarding general education does not ensure that "they" will use it. Institutions must go about establishing procedures to foster, support, and require the use of assessment information to improve general education programming as well as improvements in the majors. The systematic assessment process described, as well as how its results were utilized should be documented through the procedures outlined in the following chapter.

CHAPTER VII

DOCUMENTATION OF ASSESSMENT ACTIVITIES AND USE OF RESULTS TO IMPROVE GENERAL EDUCATION

The end result of the assessment activities described previously is the improvement of general education through a well-documented and systematic process. The key concept discussed in this brief chapter is *documentation* of this systematic process of assessment of student learning outcomes and the resulting improvement of the general education program and the learning/achievement of students.

It is absolutely necessary to create at least a minimal, but consistent, paper trail describing assessment activities regarding general education. According to one regional accrediting association employee in the Fall Semester, 1998, "If it isn't written down, it didn't happen." This is necessary because so many institutions have promised implementation of assessment and improvement activities and then failed to fulfill those promises. In many ways, the situation between institutions and their regional accrediting association is similar to that in arms reduction negotiations between President Ronald Reagan and Mr. Mikhail Gorbachev representing the former Soviet Union. In those negotiations, President Reagan said that he would "trust, but verify." Regional accrediting associations representatives will trust, but verify through a review of documentation, that assessment in general education has indeed led to program improvement.

The importance of the consistency in documentation procedures has led one of the authors to modify the statement made by the regional accrediting association representative in the Fall Semester, 1998, quoted previously to state that, "If you can't find the documentation it didn't happen." In many cases, without a consistent means for documentation across the campus, various procedures or forms for documenting the use of assessment results succeed only in concealing this use from busy accreditation visiting team members. It is as important that the use of assessment results be easily identified and located as it is that they be written down. If the accreditation team cannot find written evidence of the use of assessment results to improve learning, it will not be the members of the team that suffer.

The information presented in documentation of these activities should be concise and focused. It should relate in a systematic manner the intended general education outcomes, means of assessment, assessment results, and reports of verifiable improvements in the general education program. There is no requirement that a dissertation or thesis be prepared regarding assessment activities in general education. However, there needs to be enough information within the report to clearly show the systematic nature of the assessment procedure, convince the reader that assessment activities actually took place, and identify the specific changes in the general education programming which took place.

The responsibility for assessment documentation in general education is, as is the rest of this subject, complex. While many of the disciplines supporting general education will be engaged in improving their offerings, it should be the responsibility of the general education assessment committee to maintain the overall documentation of these program improvements. This means that committee members will need to first actively consult with the disciplines involved and then in conjunction with the committee chair prepare the documentation later described in this chapter. The documentation of assessment activities in general education should be conducted in the same manner as forms of assessment documentation concerning the institution's other instructional programs or majors.

Figure 52

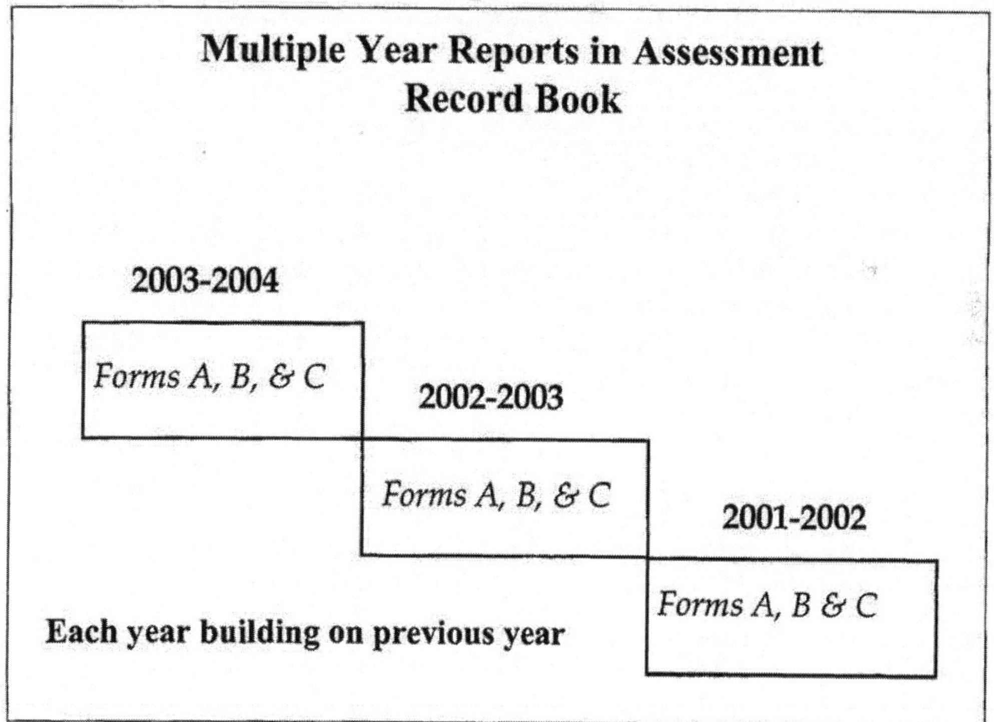

The Assessment Record Book concept and forms explained in this chapter and provided in Appendix C are recommended as one relatively simple and straightforward way to accomplish documentation. Many institutions have found these forms an easy and user-friendly way to follow the assessment process while at the same time maintaining the necessary linkage to the overall purpose of the institution.

These forms are maintained by the general education assessment committee with input from the various disciplines and enjoy the following advantages:

- They retain the linkages in the five-column model previously explained.
- They highlight the systematic nature of the assessment process by leading from the statement of purpose for the institution, to the general education program intended outcomes, means of assessment, assessment results and, finally, use of results.
- They are tightly focused to provide the minimum documentation necessary.
- They may be downloaded from the Institutional Effectiveness Associates (IEA) Internet website (www.iea-nich.com) at no cost.

The Assessment Record Book consists of three types of forms, which are provided in Appendix C. These annual reports should be accumulated as depicted in Figure 52 so that a historical record of assessment activities regarding general education is available at the time of the accreditation reaffirmation visitation. Form A constitutes little more than a cover sheet which identifies the program, in this case, general education, on which the report is provided. Form B links the general education program to the institution's expanded statement of purpose and lists the intended outcomes for the general education program during the assessment period (covering columns 1 and 2 of the five-column model, see Figures 53 and 54). Form C constitutes an assessment report concerning each intended general education outcome; its means of assessment and criteria for success (see Figure 55); a summary of the assessment data collected (see Figure 56); and a description of how this assessment information was utilized to improve the general education program (see Figure 57). Completion of these forms demonstrates the general education program's movement from planning to implementation and closing the loop. In most cases, the annual report and documentation concerning assessment activities regarding general education can be accomplished in five word-processed Assessment Record book forms each year.

Appendix C contains copies of Forms A, B, and C. It should be noted that these example pages have been reduced in size from the 8-1/2 by 11 inch standard format which comprise the Assessment Record Book. For your convenience, these forms, as well as instructions for completing them, are available for downloading from the IEA website at www.iea-nich.com. Care should be utilized in downloading to select the *instructional programs* Assessment Record Book forms found at that site into either the Microsoft Word® or Word Perfect® software on your campus.

While the primary copy of the Assessment Record Book regarding general education should be retained by the general education assessment committee, a second copy should be maintained at the institutional level to be readily available to the accreditation reaffirmation visiting team members. The second copy also serves as a backup copy should the assessment record book being maintained by the committee be misplaced.

The assessment record book procedures explained in this chapter constitute a relatively easy way to maintain the necessary documentation regarding assessment activities in general education and prevent each institution from "reinventing the wheel" regarding this subject.

Figure 53

Transition Five-Column Model to Assessment Record

General Education Program

COLUMN 1

Mission Statement:
... Community College operates in the belief that all individuals should be ... provided an opportunity to equip themselves for a fulfilling life and responsible citizenship in a world characterized by change.

Goal Statement:
Insure that all recipients of an Associate of Arts Degree will be able to:
a. Express themselves clearly and correctly in writing.
b. Read and understand literature and current event articles commonly found in the print media.
c. Perform the basic mathematical calculations required to function in society.

ASSESSMENT REPORT

FOR

_______________________   _______________________
(Instructional Degree Program)   (Degree Level)

_______________________   _______________________
(Assessment Period Covered)   (Date Submitted)

Expanded Statement of Institutional Purpose Linkage:

Institutional Mission Reference

College/University Goal(s) Supported:

Program Intended Educational (Student) Outcomes:

1.

2.

3.

4.

5.

Form B-Linkage Page

Figure 54

Transition Five-Column Model to Assessment Record

General Education Program

COLUMN 2

Program Intended Educational Outcomes:

1. Compose an essay concerning a current events topic.

2. Read with understanding.

3. Accomplish basic mathematical skills.

ASSESSMENT REPORT

FOR

_______________________   _______________________
(Instructional Degree Program)   (Degree Level)

_______________________   _______________________
(Assessment Period Covered)   (Date Submitted)

Expanded Statement of Institutional Purpose Linkage:

Institutional Mission Reference:

College/University Goal(s) Supported:

Program Intended Educational (Student) Outcomes:

1.

2.

3.

4.

5.

Form B-Linkage Page

Figure 55

Transition Five-Column Model to Assessment Record

General Education Program

COLUMN 2

Program Intended Educational Outcomes:
1. Compose an essay concerning a current events topic.

COLUMN 3

Means of Program Assessment & Criteria for Success:

1a. 80% of those writing samples selected at the end of English 202 will pass the faculty written standards rubrics. No single rubric will exhibit more than 1/4 of the students' ratings of "needs improvement" or unsatisfactory"

1b. No more than 30% of student skills scores on the "writing as a process" or the "conventions of written English" scales will be reported as "low" on the CBASE.

2a.

2b.

3

ASSESSMENT REPORT

FOR

__________________________   __________________________
(Instructional Degree Program)   (Degree Level)

__________________________   __________________________
(Assessment Period Covered)   (Date Submitted)

Intended Educational (Student) Outcome:

NOTE: There should be one Form C for each intended outcome listed on Form B. Intended outcome should be restated in the box immediately below and the intended outcome number entered in the blank spaces.

>

First Means of Assessment for Outcome Identified Above:

> **1a.** Means of Program Assessment & Criteria for Success:

> **1a.** Summary of Assessment Data Collected:

> **1a.** Use of Results to Improve Instructional Program:

Second Means of Assessment for Outcome Identified Above:

> **1b.** Means of Program Assessment & Criteria for Success:

> **1b.** Summary of Assessment Data Collected:

> **1b.** Use of Results to Improve Instructional Program:

Form C-Educational Outcome Report Page

Figure 56

Transition Five-Column Model to Assessment Record

<u>General Education Program</u>

<u>COLUMN 4</u>

<u>Summary of Data Collected:</u>

1a. 82% were found overall "acceptable" by the faculty panel. However, 41% were rated either "needs improvement" or "unacceptable" on the Thematic Organization rubric.

1b. 19% were reported as "low" on the "Writing as a Process" skill and 26% on the "Conventions of Written English" skill.

2a.

2b.

3.

Figure 57

Transition Five-Column Model to Assessment Record

General Education Program

COLUMN 5

Use of Results:

1a. "Thematic Organization" rubric now emphasized in critique of English Comp I and II classes.

1b. Match of the "Conventions of Written English" skill area on CBASE with course syllabi reviewed. Additional collaboration with "Writing Center" has doubled the number of student writing examples reviewed in Comp I & II.

2a.

2b.

3.

ASSESSMENT REPORT

FOR

________________________   ________________________
(Instructional Degree Program)   (Degree Level)

________________________   ________________________
(Assessment Period Covered)   (Date Submitted)

Intended Educational (Student) Outcome:

NOTE: There should be one Form C for each intended outcome listed on Form B. Intended outcome should be restated in the box immediately below and the intended outcome number entered in the blank spaces.

First Means of Assessment for Outcome Identified Above:

1a. Means of Program Assessment & Criteria for Success:

1a. Summary of Assessment Data Collected:

1a. Use of Results to Improve Instructional Program:

Second Means of Assessment for Outcome Identified Above:

1b. Means of Program Assessment & Criteria for Success:

1b. Summary of Assessment Data Collected:

1b. Use of Results to Improve Instructional Program:

Form C-Educational Outcome Report Page

CHAPTER VIII

FINAL COMMENTS REGARDING ASSESSMENT AND IMPROVEMENT OF GENERAL EDUCATION

As certainly as the sun rises in the East and sets in the West, your institution will be asked to demonstrate how it has assessed and improved general education. The "lessons learned" shown below are taken from the experience (often bitter) of those who have gone through this process before and are offered for your consideration.

Lessons Learned Concerning Assessment in General Education

1. Secure support from Chief Executive and Chief Academic Officers.
2. Coordinate the process through a faculty-based general education assessment committee with membership from key stakeholders.
3. Set a timeline and stick with it.
4. Choose the programmatic approach to organization.
5. Every department providing service courses may not be continually involved in assessment.
6. Limit the number of general education program outcomes being assessed at one time to no more than three to five.
7. Consider using standardized instrumentation, if time is a constraint.
8. Expect confrontation.
9. Understand that change will be gradual (glacial).
10. Document use of results thoroughly.

It is absolutely necessary to secure support from the Chief Executive and Chief Academic Officers so that they understand that which is taking place and why it is necessary. These key administrators will need to stand behind the individuals and the committee leading implementation of assessment activities in general education "when the going gets tough."

It is imperative that early faculty involvement with assessment in general education be established. This is probably best accomplished through the formation of a faculty based general education assessment committee with members from each of the key disciplines providing service courses to the general education curriculum.

Assessment implementation in general education will take roughly twice the amount of time as that in the major due to the factors earlier cited. Nonetheless, it is exceedingly important to set a timeline for each phase of activities and then to press forward to complete activities in a timely manner. The general education assessment committee, in its coordination role, should set the timeline and monitor compliance therewith by the individual disciplines. These activities can be conducted in parallel with assessment in the major and administrative and educational support units.

As tempting as it may be to approach general education assessment on a course-by-course basis, choice of the programmatic approach outlined earlier will ultimately ease the assessment burden and stands a much better chance of resulting in use of results to genuinely improve programming. In many cases, faculty can comment upon intended program outcomes more comfortably than upon the individual courses associated with those outcomes. That is so because of the direct connection of individual faculty with the courses and the vested interest, which this association brings forward.

While it may initially appear that every instructional department engaged in the provision of general education service courses should be heavily engaged in assessment activities at all times, such activity is not required and will eventually lead to exhaustion. Select three to five program outcomes and focus assessment activities on those outcomes. The fact that several of the departments providing service courses to general education are not conducting assessment activities in a given year is not a problem.

If the institution is within less than eighteen months of reaffirmation visitation, it should clearly consider use of standardized instrumentation. There simply is insufficient time during the last year to both construct and implement locally developed means of assessment in a consistent and systematic manner.

Because the subject involves areas in which most faculty have little experience with or affection for a disciplined and systematic approach to evaluation, some faculty can be expected to be quite agitated, verbal, and even hostile during the process. Leaders in the assessment of general education should expect confrontation.

It is important to understand (for one's peace of mind) that the changes suggested in general education will, in all likelihood, be very gradual. Do not expect revolutionary changes, as these changes are difficult to move through faculty governance structures, and may result in disruption of faculty staffing patterns or assignments which have evolved over decades and are considered by some as inviolable.

Because changes in the general education program will be brought about within individual service departments, an extra effort must be made to document these changes. The chair of the general education assessment committee should maintain the Assessment Record Book specifically regarding the general education program at the institution. A second copy should be maintained at the institutional level (with other ARB's) in case the copy maintained by the chair is misplaced during transition.

Assessment and improvement in general education is one of those activities that are absolutely necessary, but neither fun nor easy. It is uncomfortable, tense, and most frequently very frustrating work. However, adjustments in general education and improvement of student learning in general education will benefit a broader segment of the campus community than any other action in overall comprehensive institutional effectiveness implementation. For that reason, patience, fortitude and perseverance (along with a "thick skin") must characterize the journey upon which you and your institution now embark. Let the journey begin!

APPENDIX A

MEANS OF ASSESSMENT OFTEN ASSOCIATED WITH DIFFERING TYPES OF GENERAL EDUCATION OUTCOMES

Types of Intended General Education Outcomes Regarding:	*Associated Means of Assessment*
BASIC SKILLS	
Reading	Comprehensive Standardized Tests, Nelson-Denny, ACT ASSET
Writing	Comprehensive Standardized Tests, Portfolio, Writing Sample
Speaking	Videotaped Presentations with Standardized Evaluation Sheets
Mathematical Calculations	Comprehensive Standardized Tests, Locally Developed Examinations
Basic Computer Skills	Locally Developed Performance Tests, Commercial Computer Skills Tests (conduct Internet search)
KNOWLEDGE/UNDERSTANDING	
Historical Perspective	College BASE, Locally Developed Tests
Literary Styles	College BASE, Locally Developed Tests
Culture	Locally Developed Tests or Surveys, Observation
Meaning of Numerical Data	Locally Developed Cognitive Tests, Performance Tests
Global Perspective	Graduating Student or Alumni Surveys Employer Surveys
Impact of Technology	Graduating Student or Alumni Surveys

Types of Intended General Education Outcomes Regarding:	*Associated Means of Assessment*
HIGHER ORDER THINKING SKILLS	
Critical Thinking	Comprehensive Standardized Tests
Logical Reasoning	Watson-Glaser Critical Thinking Appraisal
Scientific/Abstract Inquiry	California Critical Thinking Skills Test
Concept Integration	TASKS in Critical Thinking
	Locally Developed Case Studies
VALUES DEVELOPMENT	
Commitment to Democratic Ideal	Graduating Student or Alumni Surveys • Voting Record • Political Activity • Attitude Toward Concepts
Cultural Diversity	Graduating Student and Alumni Surveys—Attitudes Locally Developed Case Studies
Aesthetic Appreciation	Graduating Student and Alumni Surveys • Attitudes • Reported Events Report of Voluntary Attendance at Fine Arts Presentations While Enrolled
Ethical Perspective	Graduating Student and Alumni Surveys • Attitudes • Reported Events Locally Developed Case Studies
Religious Orientation	Graduating Student and Alumni Surveys • Attitudes • Reported Events Report of Voluntary Chapel Attendance While Enrolled Locally Developed Case Studies

APPENDIX B

SUMMARY OF NATIONALLY STANDARDIZED ATTITUDINAL SURVEYS FOR ASSESSMENT OF GENERAL EDUCATION

American College Testing (ACT), the College Board in conjunction with the National Center for Higher Education Management Systems (NCHEMS), as well as the Indiana University, Center for Post-Secondary Research and Planning provide nationally standardized attitudinal surveys of potential use in assessment of general education.

The **American College Testing Program/Evaluation Survey Services (ACT/ ESS)** offers fifteen post-secondary survey instruments including the following:

- Alumni Survey
- Alumni Survey (Two-Year College Form)
- Alumni Outcomes Survey
- College Outcomes Survey
- College Student Needs Assessment Survey
- Entering Student Survey
- Student Opinion Survey
- Student Opinion Survey (Two-Year College Form)

These surveys are optically scanned, containing two to four pages of questions designed for making general evaluations of the institution's instructional and other services. Local personnel have the option of adding twenty to thirty additional questions for each of the surveys. ACT also offers a catalog of additional survey items from which institutions may select in lieu of writing individual institutional questions. In addition, each instrument provides space for the participant to write comments or suggestions. This set of surveys has been in existence since 1979 and well over a million have been distributed on college and university campuses.

The College Outcomes Survey is particularly attuned to interest in assessment of general education. This survey includes items specifically related to the institution's general education program such as "Improving my writing skills" and other outcomes. It asks students to identify the "importance" of such outcomes to their collegiate expectations as well as their "progress" in meeting those outcomes. In addition, students are asked to identify their "personal growth" and the college contribution to that growth on thirty-six items ranging from "Becoming an effective team or group member" to "Acquiring a well-rounded general education." Further information concerning the ESS Surveys may be obtained by contacting:

Post-Secondary Services
Outcomes Assessment
ACT
P.O. Box 168
Iowa City, Iowa 52243-0168
Phone: (319) 337-1051
Internet: www.act.org

The **Student Outcomes Information Service (SOIS)**, co-sponsored by the College Board and the National Center for Higher Education Management Systems, is in many respects like the ACT/ESS. The questionnaires focus on six different points during and after college:

1. Entering students
2. Continuing students
3. Program completers and graduating students
4. Former students
5. Recent Alumni
6. Three to five-year follow-up

The questionnaires, offered in formats for both two-year and four-year institutions, provide background demographics; survey educational experiences (including general education), plans, and goals; identify the need for, use of, and satisfaction with institutional services; and give perceptions and impressions of the institution as held by the various survey populations.

Perhaps the most significant difference between the SOIS and ACT/ESS families of surveys is the coordinated, research-oriented approach of the SOIS, which is supported by a carefully written handbook, *Student Outcomes Questionnaires: An Implementation Handbook* (2nd ed., 1983), by Peter T. Ewell.

Ewell takes the novice practitioner through the process step by step and carefully points out tricks and essential steps to help guarantee successful, usable survey results. As with ACT, data processing and questionnaire analyses are available. Annual summaries of information from participating institutions are also made available.

Information concerning the SOIS can be obtained by contacting:

National Center for Higher Education Management System
P.O. Drawer P
Boulder, CO 80301
Phone: (303) 497-0371
E-mail: ewellp@colorado.edu

The **College Student Experiences Questionnaire (CSEQ)** assesses the quality of effort college students expend in using the resources and opportunities provided by the institution for their learning and development. Quality of effort is reputedly the best predictor for understanding the effects of attending college because it provides an estimate of the contributions students make to their own learning as well as the resources the institution offers. A community college version is available.

The CSEQ provides:

- information about students' background and their status in college;
- an index of student satisfaction with college;
- a report on the extent of student reading and writing and involvement in other learning activities;
- student ratings of key characteristics of the college environment;
- estimates of student gains (progress) toward important objectives;
- capacity for life-long, continuous learning; and
- exposure to good practices in undergraduate education.

The section of the CSEQ related to "measures of the estimate of gains" during college is particularly relevant to assessment of general education. The estimate of gains scales consist of student ratings of progress toward important educational goals. These goals (23 of them) are commonly found in writings about higher education and have been used in national surveys over the past several decades.

The instructions for this section are as follows: "In thinking over your experience in college up to now, to what extent do you feel you have gained or made progress in each of the following respects?" The answers from which the respondent may choose are "very little," "some," "quite a bit," or "very much."

The goals are present here in five major clusters:

General Education, Literature, Arts, and Social Sciences
- broad knowledge about different fields
- understanding and enjoyment of art, music, and drama
- acquaintance with and enjoyment of literature
- awareness of different philosophies and cultures
- seeing the importance of history
- gaining the knowledge about different parts of the world

Personal Development and Social Competence
- clarifying values and ethical standards
- self-understanding
- understanding others and the ability to get along
- ability to function as a team member
- good health habits and physical fitness

Science and Technology
- understanding the nature of science
- understanding new scientific and technical developments
- becoming aware of the consequences of new applications

Intellectual Skills
- analysis and logic
- synthesis and relationships

- quantitative thinking
- independent inquiry and learning
- effective writing
- familiarity with computers

Vocational Competence

- skills for a specific job or type of work
- information broadly relevant to a career
- background and specialization for advanced education

Information concerning CSEQ can be obtained by contacting:

Indiana University
Center for Post-Secondary Research and Planning
Smith Research Center, Room 174
2805 E. 10th Street
Bloomington, IN 47408-2698
Phone: (812) 856-5825 Fax: (812) 856-5150
E-mail: CSEQ@indiana.edu

APPENDIX C

ASSESSMENT RECORD BOOK FORMS AND INSTRUCTIONS FOR COMPLETION

The *Instructions for Completion of Assessment Record Book forms for Instructional Programs* as well as Forms A, B, and C, shown (with an example of completed forms) on the following pages are available in MSWord® or Corel WordPerfect® for Windows from the Institutional Effectiveness Associates website http://www.iea-nich.com. They may be downloaded from the site without charge. For those readers not able to utilize the website, permission to photocopy, modify, and use the instructions and forms contained in this appendix is granted.

Instructions for Completion of Assessment Record Book Forms for the General Education Program

Instructions for Title Page (Form A)

- In the blank provided at the top of the page, *indicate "General Education."*
- In the blank provided, *indicate the "Assessment Period Covered" by the report that follows.* This should be indicated in months and years. For example: July 2001 – June 2002.
- In the space provided, *enter the date the assessment report was forwarded to the committee or individual responsible for assessment at the institution.* This will assist in identification of each iteration and potential refinements of the assessment report covering the same time period.
- In the space provided under "Title of Instructional Degree Programs," enter: General Education.
- In the space provided, *list the "Degree Level"* as "Undergraduate."
- In the blank provided, *enter the name of the general education assessment committee chair.*

Instructions for Linkage Page (Form B)
- The four blanks at the top of the page should have the *identical information as provided on the Title Page (Form A).*
- In the box identified as "Institutional Mission Reference," *enter all or a portion of the institutional mission that is supported by the General Education program.*
- In the box containing "College/University Goal(s) Supported," identify *which of the institution's goals the General Education program directly supports.*

- In each of the blocks listed under "Intended Educational (Student) Outcomes," *enter one of the intended educational (student) outcomes for the General Education program.*

Instructions for Intended Educational (Student) Outcome Report Pages (Form C)

- You will complete one Intended Educational (Student) Outcome Report Page (Form C) for each Intended Educational (Student) Outcome stated on Form B. Thus, if there are three "Intended Educational (Student) Outcomes" listed on the Form B, there will be three Form Cs.
- The three blanks on the top of each Form C will be *completed identically to those on Form B.*
- On your first Intended Educational (Student) Outcome Sheet (Form C), in the box underneath "Intended Educational (Student) Outcome" *transfer the first outcome from Form B.* On the second Form C transfer the second Intended Educational (Student) Outcome from Form B into the box at the top of Form C, and continue this process for all outcomes.
- Complete the boxes under the "First Means of Assessment for Outcome Identified Above" subsection according to the directions listed below:
  1. Means of Program Assessment & Criteria for Success: *Describe the .source of your assessment information.* Based on the selected means of assessment, provide a criterion for success which answers the question: "If our General Education program is functioning the way we think it 'ought' to function, what will be our score on this means of assessment?"
  2. Summary of Assessment Data Collected: Enter *a brief summary of the data you collected from your assessment activities.* There should be enough data here to convince the reader that assessment has been done. Data should be in exact figures, not rounded. Make sure the data collected relate to the intended educational (student) outcome described in the first box.
  3. Use of Results to Improve Instructional Program: *Describe how the faculty in General Education used information obtained from the assessment activities,* described in the "Means of Program Assessment and Criteria for Success" block, to improve the learning of their students. Often, this will lead to some sort of curricular change. This improvement needs to relate to the Intended Educational (Student) Outcome stated in the box at the top of the page. If the General Education program fails to meet its criteria for success then this section is used to describe what actions the faculty have taken to assure that the intended outcome is met.

- Complete the boxes under "Second Means of Assessment for Outcome Identified Above" as you completed the boxes under "First Means of Assessment for Outcome Identified Above."

ASSESSMENT RECORD FOR
DEPARTMENT
OF

____

(Academic Department Name)

_________________________   _________________________

(Assessment Period Covered)   **(Date Submitted)**

Includes Assessment Reports for those Instructional Programs listed below:

<u>Title of Instructional Degree Program</u>	<u>Degree Level</u>
_______________________	_______________
_______________________	_______________
_______________________	_______________
_______________________	_______________
_______________________	_______________
_______________________	_______________
_______________________	_______________
_______________________	_______________

Submitted By: _______________________________________

(Departmental Chair or Faculty Assessment Representative)

Form A-Title Page

ASSESSMENT RECORD FOR
DEPARTMENT
OF

<u>**General Education Program**</u>
(Academic Department Name)

September 200x – August 200x   **September 15, 200x**

(Assessment Period Covered)   (Date Submitted)

Includes Assessment Reports for those Instructional Programs listed below:

<u>**Title of Instructional Degree Program**</u>   <u>**Degree Level**</u>

                                                                                College Parallel

_______________________   _______________

_______________________   _______________

_______________________   _______________

_______________________   _______________

_______________________   _______________

_______________________   _______________

_______________________   _______________

Submitted By: _________________________________

(Departmental Chair or Faculty Assessment Representative)

Form A-Title Page

ASSESSMENT REPORT
FOR

______________________________   ______________________________
(Instructional Degree Program)   **(Degree Level)**

______________________________   ______________________________
(Assessment Period Covered)   **(Date Submitted)**

Expanded Statement of Institutional Purpose Linkage:

Institutional Mission Reference:

College/University Goal(s) Supported:

Intended Educational (Student) Outcomes:

1.

2.

3.

4.

5.

Form B-Linkage Page

ASSESSMENT REPORT
FOR

General Education Program
(Instructional Degree Program)

College Parallel
(Degree Level)

September 200x-August 200x
(Assessment Period Covered)

September 15, 200x
(Date Submitted)

Expanded Statement of Institutional Purpose Linkage:

Institutional Mission Reference: ... Community College operates in the belief that all individuals should be provided an opportunity to equip themselves for a fulfilling life and responsible citizenship in a world characterized by change.

College/University Goal(s) Supported: Insure that all recipients of an Associate of Arts Degree will be able to: a. Express themselves clearly and correctly in writing. b. Read and understand literature and current event articles commonly found in the print media. c. Perform the basic mathematical calculations required to function in society.

Program Intended Educational (Student) Outcomes:

1. Compose an essay concerning a current events topic.

2. Read with understanding.

3. Accomplish basic mathematical skills.

4.

5.

Form B-Linkage Page

ASSESSMENT REPORT
FOR

(Instructional Degree Program)	**(Degree Level)**
(Period Covered)	**(Date Submitted)**

Intended Educational (Student) Outcome:

NOTE: There should be one form C for each intended outcome listed on form B. Intended outcome should be restated in the box immediately below and the intended outcome number entered in the blank spaces.

First Means of Assessment for Outcome Identified Above:

___ a. Means of Program Assessment & Criteria for Success:

___ a. Summary of Assessment Data Collected:

___ a. Use of Results to Improve Instructional Program:

Second Means of Assessment for Outcome Identified Above:

___ b. Means of Program Assessment & Criteria for Success:

___ b. Summary of Assessment Data Collected:

___ b. Use of Results to Improve Instructional Program:

Form C

ASSESSMENT REPORT
FOR

General Education Program	*College Parallel*
(Instructional Degree Program)	**(Degree Level)**

September 200x-August 200x	**September 15, 200x**
(Period Covered)	**(Date Submitted)**

Intended Educational (Student) Outcome:

NOTE: There should be one form C for each intended outcome listed on form B. Intended outcome should be restated in the box immediately below and the intended outcome number entered in the blank spaces.

1.	Compose an essay concerning a current events topic.

First Means of Assessment for Outcome Identified Above:

_1 a. Means of Program Assessment & Criteria for Success: 80% of those writing samples selected at the end of English 202 will pass the faculty written standards rubrics. No single rubric will exhibit more than 1/4 of the students" ratings of "needs improvement" or "unsatisfactory."

_1 a. Summary of Assessment Data Collected: 82% were found overall "acceptable" by the faculty panel. However, 41% were rated either "needs improvement" or "unacceptable" on the Thematic Organization rubric.

_1 a. Use of Results to Improve Instructional Program: "Thematic Organization" rubric now emphasized in critique of English Comp I and II classes.

Second Means of Assessment for Outcome Identified Above:

_1 b. Means of Program Assessment & Criteria for Success: No more than 30% of those student skills scores on the "Writing as a Process" or the "Conventions of Written English" will be reported as "low" on the College BASE.

_1 b. Summary of Assessment Data Collected: 19% were reported as "low" on the "Writing as a Process" skill and 26% on the "Conventions of Written English" skill.

_1 b. Use of Results to Improve Instructional Program: Match of the "Conventions of Written English" skill area on CBASE with course syllabi reviewed. Additional collaboration with "writing center" has doubled the number of students writing examples reviewed in Comp I & II.

Form C-Educational Outcome Report Page

ASSESSMENT REPORT
FOR

General Education Program	*College Parallel*
(Instructional Degree Program)	**(Degree Level)**
September 200x-August 200x	**September 15, 200x**
(Period Covered)	**(Date Submitted)**

Intended Educational (Student) Outcome:

NOTE: There should be one form C for each intended outcome listed on form B. Intended outcome should be restated in the box immediately below and the intended outcome number entered in the blank spaces.

> 2. Read with understanding.

First Means of Assessment for Outcome Identified Above:

> **_2 a. Means of Program Assessment & Criteria for Success:** Combined "high" and "medium"reported skills scores in "reading critically" will comprise 80% of those taking the College BASE.

> **_2 a. Summary of Assessment Data Collected:** 61% of scores were reported in the "high" or "medium" range.

> **_2 a. Use of Results to Improve Instructional Program:** History 106, Literature 105, Political Science 202, modified to require students on several occasions to read a passage critically recognizing assumptions and implications, and evaluating ideas.

Second Means of Assessment for Outcome Identified Above:

> **_2 b. Means of Program Assessment & Criteria for Success:**Combined "high" and "medium" reported skills scores in "Reading Analytically" will comprise 75% of those taking the College BASE.

> **_2 b. Summary of Assessment Data Collected:** 78% of the scores on the "Reading Analytically" skills score were reported to be in the "high" or "medium" range.

> **_2 b. Use of Results to Improve Instructional Program:** No action this academic year, continue to monitor.

Form C-Educational Outcome Report Page

ASSESSMENT REPORT
FOR

General Education Program	*College Parallel*
(Instructional Degree Program)	**(Degree Level)**

September 200x-August 200x	September 15, 200x
(Period Covered)	**(Date Submitted)**

Intended Educational (Student) Outcome:

NOTE: There should be one form C for each intended outcome listed on form B. Intended outcome should be restated in the box immediately below and the intended outcome number entered in the blank spaces.

3. Accomplish basic mathematical skills.

First Means of Assessment for Outcome Identified Above:

_3 a. Means of Program Assessment & Criteria for Success: An average of at least 300 will be achieved on "General Mathematics" component of the College BASE examination and no more than 35% of the skill scores reported on any of its areas will be "low".

_3 a. Summary of Assessment Data Collected: The average score on the "General Mathematics" cluster was reported as 327. However, 27% of students scores were reported as being "low" in the "Using Statistics" skill area.

_3 a. Use of Results to Improve Instructional Program: Math 107, Quantitative Reasoning, is now required for all college parallel students

Second Means of Assessment for Outcome Identified Above:

_3 b. Means of Program Assessment & Criteria for Success:

_3 b. Summary of Assessment Data Collected:

_3 b. Use of Results to Improve Instructional Program:.

Form C-Educational Outcome Report Page

Made in the USA
Monee, IL
08 July 2026

56693584R00067